50 FRENCH COFFEE BREAKS

SHORT ACTIVITIES TO IMPROVE YOUR FRENCH
ONE CUP AT A TIME

COFFEE BREAK LANGUAGES

Introduction by
MARK PENTLETON

Series Editor
AVA DINWOODIE

CoffeeBreak
French

First published by Teach Yourself in 2022
An imprint of John Murray Press
A division of Hodder & Stoughton Ltd,
An Hachette UK company

13

A CIP catalogue record for this title is available from the British Library

Paperback ISBN 9781399802369
eBook ISBN 9781399802376

Typeset by KnowledgeWorks Global Ltd.

Printed and bound in Great Britain by Clays Ltd, Elcograf S.p.A.

John Murray Press policy is to use papers that are natural, renewable and
recyclable products and made from wood grown in sustainable forests.
The logging and manufacturing processes are expected to conform to the
environmental regulations of the country of origin.

John Murray Press
Carmelite House
50 Victoria Embankment
London EC4Y 0DZ

Nicholas Brealey Publishing
Hachette Book Group
Market Place, Center 53, State Street
Boston, MA 02109, USA

www.teachyourself.com

CONTENTS

ÇA TE DIRAIT UN PETIT CAFÉ ?

Bonjour ! Ça te dirait un petit café ? Fancy a coffee? This book is designed to make it easy for you to learn just a little bit of French every single time you take a Coffee Break.

It is divided into three sections, so that you can decide how long you've got and choose an activity that will fill whatever time you have. Is it just a quick **expresso**? A little longer for a **café allongé** or a **grand crème**? Or do you have time for **un éclair** to go with that? Whether you have 5, 10 or 15 minutes for your Coffee Break today, we have something to accompany your refreshment.

Throughout the book you will find a variety of activities, including reading texts, grammar exercises, writing tasks, idiom explanations and vocabulary practice.

Simply decide how long you have, choose an activity from either the 5-, 10- or 15-minute Coffee Break section and start learning. **C'est parti !**

ABOUT COFFEE BREAK LANGUAGES

Coffee Break Languages came into being in 2006 with the launch of the Coffee Break Spanish podcast. As the first podcast for beginners in Spanish, the idea of "learning a language on your coffee break" quickly took off, and soon learners around the world were using the Coffee Break Languages podcasts and online courses to build their language skills.

Since then the Coffee Break method has grown to cover seven languages and has been recognised through numerous awards, including European Professional Podcast of the Year and the European Award for Languages.

The Coffee Break Languages team of language experts, teachers and native speakers is led by Mark Pentleton. A former high school languages teacher himself, Mark continues to share his passion for language learning, and the opportunities it provides, with learners around the world through podcasts, videos, courses and books.

INTRODUCTION
THE IMPORTANCE OF PRACTICE

MARK PENTLETON

"You've got to learn your instrument. Then you practise, practise, practise".

It was the virtuoso jazz saxophonist Charlie Parker who outlined the importance of practice in this way. Indeed, in a 1954 interview with fellow musician Paul Desmond, he explained that, over the course of three or four years, he would spend up to 15 hours a day practising. This allowed him to master the improvisation skills which then led to the development of Bebop and influenced countless musicians who came after him.

No matter what skill you are acquiring, regular practice plays a crucial part. And don't worry, we're not suggesting 15 hours a day! You may well bake several hundred croissants before becoming confident in your ability to master the recipe. If you're doing the Couch to 5K running plan, you need to train regularly before you're ready to tackle those 5,000 metres. And if your child happens to be learning to play the violin, then the old adage of "practice makes perfect" is probably something you say on a daily basis.

Your "instrument" is the French language. You can already play some notes on the instrument, and perhaps you can even manage a few tunes. You're probably at the stage now of wanting to "perform" these tunes, using the French you know in spoken and written situations, and perhaps even move on to more complex pieces. But before you reach this stage, there's something you must do. You've guessed it: practise!

As I said, there's no need to follow the same intense practice schedule of Charlie Parker, spending many hours a day on your language skills. Indeed, since our very first Coffee Break Languages lesson back in 2006, we've stressed the importance of "little and often" when it comes to improving your language skills. And that's exactly what this book is about.

We've brought together a collection of interesting and enjoyable exercises which will help you build your vocabulary, increase your understanding of grammar and develop a cultural awareness, all within the space of a "coffee break".

Through the exercises, you'll learn new words, see examples of grammar points that you know and learn new constructions. You'll complete reading challenges, acquire new idiomatic expressions and learn to describe what you see in a photo, a skill which you can take into your daily life and practise your language wherever and whenever you want.

If you're training for a marathon, there's no doubt that the practice you put in beforehand is hard work. But language learning is not a marathon: it's a stroll in the park, a walk along a beach at sunset, or a drive along a beautiful lakeside as the early-morning mist clears. By ensuring that your practice is enjoyable, you'll make faster progress and you'll benefit from deeper learning. And that's exactly why we've written this book of fun and engaging exercises.

I started the introduction to this book with a quotation by Charlie Parker. However, I didn't give the full quotation. Having established the fact that, after learning the basics, what you need to do to master an instrument is "practise, practise, practise", Charlie Parker went on to add a third stage in this process:

> "And then, when you finally get up there on the bandstand, forget all that and just wail".

That, in a sense, is what we're all aiming for as language learners. Of course, "wailing" may sound unpleasant and conjure up images of tears and despair, but in the context of jazz music, Parker was suggesting that if you've learned the tune and practised over and over again, then you are ready to fly, enjoying the moment and letting the music flow naturally. Having completed all of the exercises in this book, I hope that you feel ready to "fly", "wail" or simply enjoy the moment, letting your language flow naturally using the new words, phrases and grammar points you've practised.

So, all you need to do now is decide how long you'd like to spend on your French today, pick any of our coffee-break-length exercises, and begin your practice. I wish you "happy language learning" and, of course, "happy coffee breaking"!

HOW TO USE THIS BOOK

The activities in this book vary slightly in their difficulty from one to the next, but are generally around lower intermediate level, or A2–B1 on the CEFR. Remember that even if you find a particular activity a little easier, consolidation is a vital part of language learning and no learning is ever wasted.

ABBREVIATIONS

It may also help to familiarise yourself with a few abbreviations and features that you'll find throughout the book:

(m) - masculine noun

(f) - feminine noun

(m, pl) - masculine plural noun

(f, pl) - feminine plural noun

< - This introduces the infinitive form of a conjugated verb.

✎_____ - This pencil followed by a line indicates a space for you to write your answers, but feel free to add your own notes in any blank spaces on the pages too.

CHECKLISTS

At the start of each of the three sections of the book you have a checklist, where you can keep track of your Coffee Breaks by ticking off activities as you complete them.

ANSWERS SECTIONS

At the end of each activity, we'll let you know which page to turn to if there is a corresponding answers section. Remember that the learning doesn't stop when you finish writing your answers to an activity, as there is so much more to be learned by reading the answers and any extra examples or explanations that may be included there. As always, if there are words or phrases that are unfamiliar to you, remember to use your dictionary to help you. You could use any blank space on the page or your own notebook to write down this new vocabulary and help you remember it. There are also some lined pages at the back of this book where you can write your own notes.

TYPES OF ACTIVITY

Each of the three sections of this book contains a number of different types of activity. Below, you'll find a description of each type, so that you know what to expect every time you choose an activity. Whether you're looking for some grammar revision, some reading practice, a writing task, or something else, we hope that these descriptions help you to decide how you're going to spend each Coffee Break.

5-MINUTE COFFEE BREAKS

Word Builder

In these activities, you will learn some interesting pieces of vocabulary on a variety of topics. There is then a short exercise to allow you to practise this vocabulary in context. To make the most of the Word Builder activities, we recommend writing down the words that are new to you in your own notes to help you remember them.

Mini Grammar Challenge

These challenges are designed to give you a little extra practice of some tricky French grammar points. Each activity will focus on one specific point and will include a brief explanation, an exercise and answers. Don't worry if some of the grammar points are unfamiliar to you. If you would like to review any of the points covered in more detail, see the "Coffee Break lessons" section on page 227.

Idiomatically Speaking

In each of these activities, we will focus on one French idiomatic expression. First, we will explain the meaning of it and provide some examples of some of the contexts in which the idiom can be used. Then, there will be a space for you to practise using the idiom in your own sentences.

Say What You See

In these writing activities, we will provide some suggested phrases to help you write a description of an image. As there is no set answer for this type of exercise, you may not know whether or not what you've written is entirely correct. Don't worry about this too much, however, as the purpose of these writing activities is simply to get you writing freely in French, practising creating different types of texts and, in this way, developing your writing skills. For these activities, we have included our own "answer", which we hope you will find useful to see. However, it's important to remember that there is no single correct answer, so don't worry if your description is very different.

Guided Translation

Each of these activities is based on a short piece of text in French: a famous quote, a proverb or an idiom. We will talk you through the language used in the piece of text to examine in detail the vocabulary and structures used and to help you come up with a good translation of it.

10-MINUTE COFFEE BREAKS

Translation Challenge

In these activities, your challenge is to translate sentences from English into French. There will be hints to help you, if you need them, and suggested translations and language explanations in the answers section.

Famous French Speakers

These are designed to help you develop both your reading skills and your cultural knowledge. They are based on texts about famous French speakers and include a vocabulary list and questions to help you test your understanding of the text.

Jumbled Letters

In these activities, you will be given a definition of a word in French and an anagram. Your task is to unscramble the letters of the anagram to find the word being defined. Then, test your knowledge of the language by seeing how many other French words you can make using those letters.

Number Focus

It takes a while, when learning a language, to reach the stage where you can instantly visualise the corresponding digit when you hear a number being said out loud. This can only become easier with practice, which is why our Number Focus activities include a variety of exercises, all designed to help you practise your numbers in French.

Taste Bud Tantaliser

These activities use recipes as reading texts and include a vocabulary list and a reading comprehension or language exercise, so that you can practise your language skills while learning about a dish from somewhere in the French-speaking world. While the activity should only take around 10 minutes, there's nothing stopping you from getting to know the language in the recipe even better by following it and making the dish yourself when you have more time!

15-MINUTE COFFEE BREAKS

Reading Focus

These longer reading activities will allow you to study a short text about a particular aspect of French-speaking cultures. They include a vocabulary list, comprehension questions and language questions.

Guided Writing

This type of activity is designed to get you writing different kinds of texts in French. They begin with an example of a certain type of writing, from which you can draw ideas and structures. There are also suggested phrases provided to help you write your own paragraph in a similar style.

Vocabulary Consolidation

This is a vocabulary drill exercise that will help you to familiarise yourself with pieces of vocabulary on a specific topic. Each activity focuses on 20 pieces of vocabulary and includes a number of different exercises to help you practise and get to know them.

Grammar Focus

While the 5-minute Mini Grammar Challenges are perfect for a short bit of practice of specific grammar points, in these Grammar Focus activities we take a more in-depth look at different topics in French grammar, providing a more detailed explanation and a number of different exercises to help you practise. If you would like further explanation of any of the language points covered, you can find out how to do this in the "Coffee Break lessons" section on page 227.

5-MINUTE COFFEE BREAKS

CHECKLIST
5-MINUTE COFFEE BREAKS

Word Builder

Mini Grammar Challenge

Idiomatically Speaking

Say What You See

Guided Translation

1

EN ROUTE
WORD BUILDER

In this Word Builder, we're going to become more familiar with some of those all-important practical words that you'll need when you're next travelling in a French-speaking area. Read through the vocabulary list below and note down the words that are new to you to help you remember them. Then, complete the exercise that follows to practise using them.

* * *

le billet - ticket (usually for train, aeroplane)
le ticket - ticket (usually for underground, subway, bus)
le quai - platform
la porte d'embarquement - boarding gate, departure gate
l'horaire (f) - timetable
l'arrêt (m) - stop
la destination - destination
le covoiturage - carpooling
faire de l'autostop (m) - hitch-hiking

être à l'heure - to be on time
être en avance - to be early
être en retard - to be late

Now it's over to you! On the lines below, describe one of your travel experiences. Try to include at least three of these pieces of vocabulary. **C'est parti !**

_____

_____

_____

_____

_____

_____

_____

_____

_____

2

LE PASSÉ COMPOSÉ : ADVERBES
MINI GRAMMAR CHALLENGE

In this Mini Grammar Challenge, we're going to practise placing adverbs in the correct position in the perfect tense. Read the short explanation below, then practise this by completing the exercise that follows.

* * *

In the perfect tense, certain adverbs are placed between the auxiliary verb and the past participle. For example:

La ville a beaucoup changé.
The city has changed a lot.

Here, the adverb **beaucoup** is placed between the auxiliary verb **a** and the past participle **changé**.

EXERCISE

Rewrite the following sentences in the perfect tense, paying attention to the placement of the adverbs. Some of the verbs will take the auxiliary verb **être**, so watch out for the agreement of the past participle in these cases.

We've done the first one for you:

> Il parle trop.
> *Il a trop parlé.*

1. Le bébé dort bien.
   ✎ _____

   _____

2. Je mange trop.
   ✎ _____

   _____

3. Tu apprends beaucoup.
   ✎ _____

   _____

4. Nous travaillons assez.
   ✎ _____

   _____

5. Ils se comprennent mal.
   ✎ _____

   _____

6. Vous voyagez souvent.
   ✎ _____

   _____

7. Le spectacle commence déjà.

   ✎ _____

   _____

8. Elle se comporte bien.

   ✎ _____

   _____

9. Elles vont souvent en France.

   ✎ _____

   _____

10. Les enfants se réveillent déjà.

   ✎ _____

   _____

* * *

Bravo ! When you're ready, the answers can be found on page 58.

3

QUAND LES POULES AURONT DES DENTS

IDIOMATICALLY SPEAKING

The focus of this activity is the wonderfully sarcastic idiomatic expression **quand les poules auront des dents**. Literally meaning "when hens will have teeth", it can be thought of as the equivalent of the British expression "when hell freezes over" or the American expression "when pigs fly". Let's take a look at some examples of this expression in context:

Tu vas te lever quand ? Quand les poules auront des dents ?
When are you going to get up? When hell freezes over?

Franchement, je crois qu'on trouvera la réponse à cette question quand les poules auront des dents.
Honestly, I think we'll find the answer to this question when pigs fly.

Quand les poules auront des dents, je me marierai.
When hell freezes over, I'll get married.

Can you come up with a few of your own examples? Use the lines below to write three of your own sentences containing this idiom.

_____

_____

_____

_____

_____

_____

_____

_____

_____

4

AU PARC

SAY WHAT YOU SEE

What's going on in the image below? On the next page, you'll find some suggested sentence starters and phrases that will help you to practise your writing skills by describing the scene below. Use the lines on the following page to write three to five sentences describing this image. **Bonne chance !**

Au parc

SUGGESTED PHRASES

il y a - there is / are
à l'avant - at the front
à l'arrière - at the back
derrière - behind
plus loin - further
à droite - on the right
à gauche - on the left
sur le côté - at the side
de chaque côté - on each side
partout - everywhere
tout le long du chemin - all along the way
les gens - people
les arbres (m, pl) - trees
le sentier - path
les baskets (f, pl) - trainers, sneakers
les manches courtes (f, pl) - short sleeves
la poussette - pram, stroller
les lampadaires (f, pl) - streetlights, streetlamps
l'herbe (f) - grass
de l'ombre - some shade
une balade - a walk
se trouver - to be, to stand, to sit
prendre l'air - to get some fresh air
tourner le dos - to turn one's back
faire du jogging - to jog
courir - to run
faire du vélo - to cycle
vers - towards

Au parc

✎_____

_____

_____

_____

_____

_____

_____

_____

* * *

Bravo ! If you'd like to see an example answer, turn to page 59.

5

N'Y VOIR QUE DU FEU
GUIDED TRANSLATION

Have you heard the French idiom **n'y voir que du feu**? In this Guided Translation, we're going to take a look at it, word by word, in order to understand all the language used in it. **Allez, on y va !**

* * *

LANGUAGE EXPLANATION

We'll start by removing some of the tricky elements of this expression and look simply at **voir du feu**. **Voir** is, of course, the verb "to see" in its infinitive form and **du feu** literally means "some fire". **Feu** is a masculine noun, which is why it is preceded by **du** (made up of **de + le**).

Now, let's add in the negative structure which is used in this expression: **ne ... que**. In this structure, **que** is replacing the negative particle **pas**. **Ne ... que** carries the same meaning as the adverb **seulement**, "only".

Finally, what about the **y**? **Y** is a pronoun that replaces the name of a place or location and can often be translated as something like "there", "in there" or "in it". Remember that it isn't always directly translated into English. For example, we would usually translate the expression **vas-y !** or **allez-y !** simply as "go on!" or "on you go!"

Can you put all this information together and figure out the meaning of this expression?

TRANSLATION:

✎ _____

_____

* * *

When you think you know, turn to page 59 to find the answer.

6

EN VILLE
WORD BUILDER

In this Word Builder, we're focusing on a few essential reference points to help you find your way in a French-speaking town or city. Read through the vocabulary list, then have a go at the exercise that follows.

* * *

le centre commercial - shopping centre, mall
le monument - memorial, landmark
la mairie - town hall, city hall
la rivière - river (a small river that is an affluent to a bigger river)
le fleuve - river (a larger river which flows into the sea or ocean)
le trottoir - pavement, sidewalk
la banlieue - suburbs
l'arrondissement (m) - district

À vous ! Now, let's practise using this vocabulary in context. Fill in the gaps in the following sentences with the most appropriate piece of vocabulary from the list.

1. Tu peux longer ✎_____ avant de trouver un pont pour passer de l'autre côté.
   TRANSLATION: *You can walk along* ✎_____ *before finding a bridge to get to the other side.*

2. Il faut d'abord aller à ✎_____ pour obtenir un permis de stationnement.
   TRANSLATION: *You first need to go to* ✎_____ *to get a parking permit.*

3. Ce ✎_____ sur la place du marché est en l'honneur des combattants de la Guerre 14-18.
   TRANSLATION: *This* ✎_____ *on the market square is in honour of the soldiers from the First World War.*

4. Pour s'éloigner du bruit, vous pouvez sortir de la ville et aller dans ✎_____ , où il y a de petits commerces.
   TRANSLATION: *To get away from the noise, you can leave the city and go to* ✎_____ , *where there are some small shops.*

5. Faites attention à bien rester sur ✎_____ près de cette route. Les voitures roulent vite ici.
   TRANSLATION: *Make sure you stay on*

✎_____ *near this road. The cars go fast here.*

* * *

Once you're happy with your answers, turn to page 60 to check them.

7

ADJECTIFS DÉMONSTRATIFS
MINI GRAMMAR CHALLENGE

In this grammar activity, we're practising using demonstrative adjectives: **ce, cette, cet** and **ces**. Read the short explanation below, then have a go at the exercise that follows.

* * *

Demonstrative adjectives are used when talking about "this", "these", "that" and "those". For example:

MASCULINE SINGULAR:
ce livre
this / that book

FEMININE SINGULAR:
cette fête
this / that party

MASCULINE & FEMININE PLURAL:

ces amis, ces amies

these / those friends

Note that **cet** is used before masculine singular nouns beginning with a vowel or a silent **h-**.

MASCULINE SINGULAR STARTING WITH A VOWEL /
SILENT H-:

cet animal

this / that animal

EXERCISE

Replace the definite article (**le / la / l' / les**) in each of the following sentences with the correct demonstrative adjective (**ce / cette / cet / ces**).

1. Nous avons acheté la maison.

   ✎_____

   _____

2. Tu as vu le chien ?

   ✎_____

   _____

3. Elle connaît les chansons par cœur.

   ✎_____

   _____

4. Avez-vous aimé le livre ?

   ✎_____

   _____

5. Il a trouvé l'exercice difficile.

✎ _____

_____

6. Les chaussures sont très chères.

✎ _____

_____

7. On a regardé le film hier.

✎ _____

_____

8. Ils n'ont pas lu l'article.

✎ _____

_____

9. J'ai compris la leçon.

✎ _____

_____

10. L'étudiant travaille dans un restaurant.

✎ _____

_____

* * *

Once you've had a go, turn to page 61 to check your answers.

IL FAIT UN FROID DE CANARD
IDIOMATICALLY SPEAKING

Have you ever described something as "duck cold"? Perhaps not in English, but in French you would be understood perfectly! In French, **il fait un froid de canard** is one expression that can be used to express how cold it is. Here are some examples of this idiom being used in context:

Ce n'est pas possible, il fait un froid de canard ce matin.
This can't be happening; it's absolutely freezing this morning.

Il a fait un froid de canard toute la nuit.
It was freezing cold all night.

À vous la parole ! In a few sentences, describe one of your coldest experiences using this idiom to help you.

_____

_____

_____

_____

_____

_____

_____

_____

_____

9

DANS LA CUISINE
SAY WHAT YOU SEE

Take a close look at this photo and think about how you would describe what's happening in it. Then, use the suggested sentence starters and vocabulary on the next page to help you write a short descriptive paragraph of three to five sentences.

Dans la cuisine

SUGGESTED PHRASES

on peut voir - we can see

dans la cuisine - in the kitchen

au milieu - in the middle

derrière eux - behind them

sur les étagères - on the shelves

plein/e de - full of

étalé/e sur - spread on

ils sont en train de rire / cuisiner - they are laughing / cooking

il / elle porte - he / she is wearing

il / elle a les cheveux blonds / bruns - he / she has blonde / brown hair

chacun/e - each

la chemise - shirt

le tablier - apron

le verre de vin rouge - glass of red wine

la serviette - tea towel, dish towel

la poêle - pan

le four - oven

les aliments (m, pl) - ingredients, food

les légumes frais (m, pl) - fresh vegetables

les asperges (f, pl) - asparagus

les radis (m, pl) - radishes

les citrons (m, pl) - lemons

le fromage - cheese

Dans la cuisine

✎ _____

_____

_____

_____

_____

_____

_____

_____

_____

_____

* * *

Très bien ! To see what we came up with, turn to page 62.

TOUT OBJECTIF SANS PLAN N'EST QU'UN SOUHAIT

GUIDED TRANSLATION

In this Guided Translation, we're looking at the language used in a quote by the French author Antoine de Saint-Exupéry, who wrote the famous book *Le Petit Prince*.

Tout objectif sans plan n'est qu'un souhait.

ANTOINE DE SAINT-EXUPÉRY

Tout objectif sans plan n'est qu'un souhait.

ANTOINE DE SAINT-EXUPÉRY

LANGUAGE EXPLANATION

Let's take a closer look at the language used in this quote.

We'll begin with **tout objectif**. The noun **un objectif** means "an objective" or "a goal". Since **objectif** is a masculine noun, it is preceded by the masculine form of **tout**, meaning "every".

Now, let's look at the next part of the sentence: **sans plan**. This is fairly straightforward to translate. The word **sans** means "without" and the word **plan** means "plan". Note that in French we do not need a word for "a" to say "without a plan". We can simply say **sans plan**.

Finally, let's focus on the negative structure **ne ... que**. Here, the word **que** replaces the negative particle **pas**. **Ne ... que** means "only" and the noun **un souhait** means "a wish".

Now, can you put all these elements together to figure out the meaning of this quote?

TRANSLATION:

_____

_____

_____

* * *

When you're ready, turn to page 62 to find the answer.

11

AU RESTAURANT
WORD BUILDER

Our focus for this vocabulary activity is the topic of ordering in a restaurant. The list below contains some words and phrases that will help you to add some extra detail when you're next ordering food in a francophone country. Take a moment to familiarise yourself with the words and phrases and note down any that are new to you. Then, have a go at the short exercise that follows.

* * *

la carte - menu (specifically, the piece of paper that lists the menu items)
le menu du jour - set menu (referring to the food itself, usually a three-course lunch or dinner exclusive to that day)
le plat du jour - dish of the day
le plat principal - main dish
l'accompagnement (m) - side dish
je vais prendre ... - I'll take ...

pour moi ... - I'll have ...

avec plus de ... / sans ... - with more ... / without ...

saignant / à point / bien cuit - rare / medium rare / well done (for meat)

ce sera tout - that will be all

Now, let's practise this. Imagine you're in a restaurant in a French-speaking country. Write a short script detailing what you would order from your dream menu. Try to include at least three pieces of vocabulary from the list. **Bonne chance et bon appétit !**

✎ _____

_____

_____

_____

_____

_____

_____

_____

_____

_____

12

PARTICIPES PRÉSENTS ET ADJECTIFS
MINI GRAMMAR CHALLENGE

As you gradually become more familiar with a language, you start to figure out its patterns. This can be very useful when it comes to trying to understand or use words that are new to you, as understanding the patterns of the language allows you to make informed guesses. For example, you may have noticed that there is a whole group of adjectives in French that are simply the present participle of their associated verb. Let's take a look at this language point, before putting it into practice in the exercise that follows.

* * *

Here are some examples of verbs whose present participle can be used as an adjective:

-ER VERB:
intéresser ("to interest") > **intéressant** ("interesting", present participle and adjective)

-IR VERB:

nourrir ("to feed, to nourish") > **nourrissant**
("nourishing", present participle and adjective)

-RE VERB:

suivre ("to follow") > **suivant** ("following", present
participle and adjective)

EXERCISE

In this exercise, your task is to adapt the structure of each
sentence in order to change the verb into an adjective.

Here's an example to help you. The following sentence uses
the verb **intéresser** with the direct object pronoun **me**,
meaning "to interest *me*":

L'apprentissage des langues m'intéresse beaucoup.
Language learning interests me a lot.

If we convert this sentence into one which uses the adjective
intéressant rather than the verb **intéresser**, we come up with
something like this:

**Je trouve l'apprentissage des langues très
intéressant.**
I find language learning very interesting.

À mon avis, l'apprentissage des langues est très intéressant.

In my opinion, language learning is very interesting.

Ce que je trouve très intéressant, c'est l'apprentissage des langues.

What I find very interesting is language learning.

In each sentence below, try transforming the verb into an adjective and adapt the sentence accordingly.

1. Ce concert m'a épaté !

   (**épater** - "to impress, to amaze")

   TRANSLATION: *That concert impressed me!*

   ✎_____

   _____

   _____

2. Le bruit du trafic m'assourdit au point que je ne vous entends pas. (**assourdir** - "to deafen")

   TRANSLATION: *The noise of the traffic is deafening me so much that I can't hear you.*

   ✎_____

   _____

   _____

3. Paul sourit toujours et ne semble jamais être de mauvaise humeur. (**sourire** - "to smile")

   TRANSLATION: *Paul is always smiling and never seems to be in a bad mood.*

   ✎_____

_____

_____

* * *

Once you've finished, the answers and further explanations can be found on page 62.

13

AVOIR LE CAFARD
IDIOMATICALLY SPEAKING

Literally meaning "to have the cockroach", **avoir le cafard** is another interesting French animal idiom. **Avoir le cafard** means "to feel down, low, blue". It can be used in many different situations and can illustrate either mild or intense sadness. Let's take a look at some examples:

Il avait l'air d'avoir le cafard hier.
He seemed to have the blues yesterday.

Toute cette discussion nous a donné le cafard.
This whole discussion got us down.

Je ne sais pas ce que j'ai, mais j'ai vraiment le cafard.
I don't know what's up with me, but I feel down in the dumps.

Can you come up with more examples using **avoir le cafard**? Try using some different tenses for an extra challenge. **On y va !**

_____

_____

_____

_____

_____

_____

_____

_____

_____

14

EN COURS
SAY WHAT YOU SEE

In this activity, we're focusing on writing skills. Take a close look at the image below, then use the suggested phrases on the next page to help you write a short description of the scene. **Allons-y !**

SUGGESTED PHRASES

la classe - classroom
le cours de maths / mathématiques - maths class
devant - at the front
au fond - at the back
l'enseignante / l'institutrice / la maîtresse - (female) teacher
les élèves (m/f, pl) - students
donner cours - to teach (a lesson)
être debout - to stand
être assis/e - to sit
lever le doigt / la main - to raise one's hand, to put up one's hand
pointer du doigt - to point one's finger
répondre à la question - to answer the question
connaître la réponse - to know the answer
elle sourit / elle est souriante - she is smiling
ils sont attentifs / sages / enthousiastes - they are alert / well-behaved / enthusiastic
les calculs (m, pl) - calculations
le cahier - notebook
le bureau - desk
le tableau - board
le gilet - cardigan

En cours

✎ _____

_____

_____

_____

_____

_____

_____

_____

_____

_____

_____

* * *

If you'd like to see what we came up with, turn to page 63.

15

APPRENDRE À UN VIEUX SINGE À FAIRE LA GRIMACE
GUIDED TRANSLATION

Are you familiar with the French proverb **ce n'est pas à un vieux singe qu'on apprend à faire la grimace**? Let's break it down word by word to get a better understanding of the language it contains.

* * *

LANGUAGE EXPLANATION

Let's start with **ce n'est pas.** You will be familiar with the French expression **c'est,** meaning "it is". In order to make the statement negative, we need to place the word **ne** before the verb and then the word **pas** after the verb. **Ne** changes to **n'** when the word that follows begins with a vowel. Therefore, **ce n'est pas** means "it is not".

Now, let's consider the construction **apprendre à quelqu'un à faire quelque chose,** which means "to teach someone how to do something". Here, the verb **apprendre** is in the third person singular form, **on apprend**, meaning "one teaches". The relative pronoun **que** means "that" and becomes **qu'** before a vowel.

Who is being taught? **Un vieux singe.** The masculine noun **singe** means "monkey". In French, adjectives tend to come after the noun. However, the adjective **vieux**, meaning "old", is an example of an adjective that comes before the noun.

Lastly, the expression **faire la grimace** means "to make faces".

Can you put all the parts of this proverb together to figure out its meaning?

TRANSLATION:

✎ _____

_____

_____

* * *

Once you're ready, turn to page 64 to read the translation and explanation.

16

OBJETS DU QUOTIDIEN
WORD BUILDER

Sometimes, when learning a language, it can be easy to forget to learn some of the most everyday vocabulary. The list below contains a few words which will help you to find your way around a French-speaking household. Read through it, noting down any words that are new to you, then have a go at the exercise that follows. **On y va !**

* * *

le parapluie - umbrella
le lave-linge - washing machine
l'aspirateur (m) - vacuum cleaner
le sèche-cheveux - hairdryer
l'oreiller (m) - pillow
l'ordinateur (m) - computer
la poubelle - bin, trash can
le robinet - tap, faucet

la cafetière - coffee maker
le congélateur - freezer
le four - oven
le micro-ondes - microwave
les couverts (m, pl) - cutlery
les mouchoirs (m, pl) - tissues
l'essuie-tout (m) - paper towel

Now, let's practise some of these. If these objects could talk, can you figure out which five would be describing themselves?

1. Quand on m'ouvre, je verse de l'eau pour laver les casseroles, les légumes, ou bien pour vous remplir votre verre d'eau. Qui suis-je ?

   ✎ _____

2. Je conserve les aliments dans le froid pendant très longtemps. Vous avez envie de glaçons pour votre limonade ? J'en ai !

   ✎ _____

3. Je sers à réchauffer des soupes, des chocolats chauds ou même des plats surgelés, de manière très rapide et efficace. Je suis ... ?

   ✎ _____

4. Tout ce que vous ne voulez plus, je veux le prendre. Je garde tous vos déchets. Je suis souvent dans la cuisine, et je dois sortir généralement une fois par semaine.

   ✎ _____

5. Je vous donne une réponse à toutes vos questions, je suis un écran vers le monde entier. Vous pouvez travailler, communiquer ou vous divertir grâce à moi.

_____

* * *

Once you're ready, turn to page 65 to check your answers.

17

PRONOMS RELATIFS
MINI GRAMMAR CHALLENGE

In this activity, we're going to practise using the relative pronouns **qui** and **que**. These are words that are used to join two parts of a sentence together. Read the explanation below to help you with the exercise that follows. **Allez, c'est parti !**

* * *

The relative pronoun **qui** can mean "who", "which" or "that". **Qui** is used when we are referring to the *subject* of the sentence: the thing that carries out the action of the verb. In most situations, **qui** is immediately followed by a verb. In the following example, **qui** refers to **le livre**, which is the subject of the verb **être**.

> **Je lis un livre. Le livre est très bon.**
> → **Je lis un livre qui est très bon.**
> → *I am reading a book that is very good.*

The relative pronoun **que** can mean "which", "that" or "whom". **Que** is used when we are referring to the *object* of the sentence: the thing that receives the action of the verb. In most situations, **que** is immediately followed by a pronoun or noun. In the following example, **que** is followed immediately by the subject pronoun **je** and refers to **le livre**, which, this time, is the object of the verb **lire**.

> **Le livre est très bon. Je lis le livre.**
> → **Le livre que je lis est très bon.**
> → *The book that I am reading is very good.*

Note that **que** becomes **qu'** before a vowel, whereas **qui** stays the same when it precedes a vowel.

EXERCISE

Complete the following sentences with the correct relative pronoun (**qui, que** or **qu'**).

1. Paris est la ville ✎_____ elle aime le plus.
2. La maison ✎_____ nous allons acheter est près du supermarché.
3. La dame ✎_____ habite ici est très gentille.
4. Tu connais le chef ✎_____ travaille dans ce restaurant ?
5. Le film ✎_____ on a vu l'autre jour était très intéressant.
6. Le rêve ✎_____ j'ai fait hier soir était vraiment bizarre.

7. Il y a des fleurs ✎_____ poussent dans le jardin.

8. Le modèle ✎_____ vous voulez n'est plus disponible.

9. Ce sont les voisins ✎_____ viennent dîner ce soir.

10. La ville ✎_____ nous visitons est charmante.

* * *

Once you're happy with your answers, you can check them on page 65.

18

AVOIR LE COUP DE FOUDRE
IDIOMATICALLY SPEAKING

French is often perceived as a romantic language, so it only makes sense that there exists a strong idiom for falling in love! **Avoir le coup de foudre** or **avoir un coup de foudre** literally means "to have a lightning strike". It's a way of expressing a sudden, intense feeling of falling in love. Here are some examples in context:

Martine a tout de suite eu un coup de foudre pour Denis.
Martine immediately fell for Denis.

Je ne crois pas que ce sera le coup de foudre entre eux deux.
I don't think it will be love at first sight between the two of them.

Je n'ai pas pu m'empêcher d'acheter ces chaussures : j'ai le coup de foudre !

I couldn't resist buying these shoes: I'm in love!

As you can see, this expression can be used in a variety of situations. Can you think of a few examples of your own? **C'est parti !**

_____

_____

_____

_____

_____

_____

_____

_____

19

AU CAFÉ

SAY WHAT YOU SEE

How would you describe what's going on in this photo? Use the suggested phrases and vocabulary on the next page to help you write three to five sentences about what you can see. **Allez, c'est parti !**

Au café

SUGGESTED PHRASES

devant - at the front

au fond - at the back

au centre - at the centre

à sa droite - to his / her right

à sa gauche - to his / her left

les amis - the friends

la terrasse d'un café - street café, outside area of a café

en plein air - in the open, outdoors

à table - at the table

rire ensemble - to laugh together

la main sur l'épaule - hand on the shoulder

porter un chapeau - to wear a hat

elle porte de grandes lunettes - she's wearing big glasses

il fait beau - the weather is nice

un t-shirt à rayures - a striped T-shirt

les habits (m, pl) **légers** - light clothes

les panneaux (m, pl) - boards, signs

sur la table - on the table

les tasses (f, pl) - cups

la tablette - tablet

le bouquet de fleurs - bunch of flowers

***

When you're ready, turn to page 66 to see an example answer.

20

LES ARBRES QUI GRANDISSENT LE PLUS LENTEMENT
GUIDED TRANSLATION

This Guided Translation will take you through the language used in a quote by Jean-Baptiste Poquelin, better known by his stage name, Molière. His quote reminds us of the rewards that perseverance can bring.

Les arbres qui grandissent le plus lentement sont ceux qui portent les meilleurs fruits.

MOLIÈRE

Les arbres qui grandissent le plus lentement sont ceux qui portent les meilleurs fruits.

MOLIÈRE

LANGUAGE EXPLANATION

Now, let's take a closer look at the language.

Grandissent comes from the verb **grandir** ("to grow"). You may recognise the verb ending **-issent** from other regular **-ir** verbs in the present tense. The subject of the verb, **les arbres** ("the trees"), is connected to **grandissent** by the relative pronoun **qui**, in this context meaning "that".

Lentement is an adverb, meaning "slowly". Here, the adverb is put into the superlative form by adding **le plus** before it. **Le plus lentement** therefore literally means "the most slowly".

Ceux qui brings us to a slightly more complicated grammar point, but put most simply it can be thought of as meaning "those that". You may find it interesting to note that **ceux** is in its masculine plural form in order to agree with **les arbres** (m, pl).

Portent is fairly easily identifiable as the third person plural form of **porter** in the present tense. However, it's not so easy to translate, as the verb can carry a number of different meanings. Can you guess from the context how **porter** would best be translated in this quote?

Les meilleurs fruits isn't too tricky to translate. We have another superlative, which is formed using the word **meilleur** ("best"). However, do you know why we are using **meilleur** rather than **mieux**?

Now, try putting all this information together and see if you can figure out what this quote from Molière means.

TRANSLATION:

✎ _____

_____

_____

* * *

When you think you know, turn to page 66 to find the translation.

57

LE PASSÉ COMPOSÉ : ADVERBES
Mini Grammar Challenge

1. Le bébé a bien dormi.
2. J'ai trop mangé.
3. Tu as beaucoup appris.
4. Nous avons assez travaillé.
5. Ils se sont mal compris.
6. Vous avez souvent voyagé.
7. Le spectacle a déjà commencé.
8. Elle s'est bien comportée.
9. Elles sont souvent allées en France.
10. Les enfants se sont déjà réveillés/ées.

AU PARC
Say What You See

Il y a des gens sur le sentier d'un parc. Il fait beau, le soleil brille et les feuilles sur les arbres sont vertes. Au premier plan, sur le sentier, une femme et un homme font du jogging. Ils sont en short de sport et en baskets. Un peu plus loin, un homme en chemise à manches courtes fait du vélo. À droite, une maman et une jeune fille se penchent vers la poussette pour parler au bébé. Derrière elles, il y a encore des gens en balade, à pied et à vélo, qui vont dans des directions différentes. À gauche, tout le long du chemin, il y a des lampadaires. Les arbres donnent de l'ombre aux promeneurs.

N'Y VOIR QUE DU FEU
Guided Translation

The literal translation of **n'y voir que du feu** is "to see only fire (there)" or "to see nothing but fire (in it)".

It is an interesting idiom, as it doesn't have a direct equivalent in English, but it means that somebody is completely clueless or oblivious to something, or that they haven't noticed something that is right in front of their eyes.

Here's an example of the idiom in context:

> **Claire n'est pas toujours très discrète à chaque fois qu'elle rentre tard, mais heureusement sa mère n'y voit que du feu.**

This could be translated in a number of ways in English, for example:

> *Claire isn't always very discreet every time she comes home late, but luckily her mother is completely clueless / oblivious / doesn't notice a thing / it goes right over her mother's head.*

We hope this has helped you to understand the meaning of the idiom **n'y voir que du feu**. During your next Coffee Break, why not choose one of the writing activities and try to use this idiom in your own writing? **Bonne chance !**

EN VILLE
Word Builder

1. Tu peux longer **la rivière / le fleuve** avant de trouver un pont pour passer de l'autre côté.
   TRANSLATION: *You can walk along **the river** before finding a bridge to get to the other side.*
2. Il faut d'abord aller à **la mairie** pour obtenir un permis de stationnement.
   TRANSLATION: *You first need to go to **the town hall** to get a parking permit.*

3. Ce **monument** sur la place du marché est en l'honneur des combattants de la Guerre 14-18.

   TRANSLATION: *This **memorial** on the market square is in honour of the soldiers from the First World War.*

4. Pour s'éloigner du bruit, vous pouvez sortir de la ville et aller dans **la banlieue**, où il y a de petits commerces.

   TRANSLATION: *To get away from the noise, you can leave the city and go to **the suburbs**, where there are some small shops.*

5. Faites attention à bien rester sur **le trottoir** près de cette route. Les voitures roulent vite ici.

   TRANSLATION: *Make sure you stay on **the pavement** near this road. The cars go fast here.*

ADJECTIFS DÉMONSTRATIFS
Mini Grammar Challenge

1. Nous avons acheté **cette** maison.
2. Tu as vu **ce** chien ?
3. Elle connaît **ces** chansons par cœur.
4. Avez-vous aimé **ce** livre ?
5. Il a trouvé **cet** exercice difficile.
6. **Ces** chaussures sont très chères.
7. On a regardé **ce** film hier.
8. Ils n'ont pas lu **cet** article.
9. J'ai compris **cette** leçon.
10. **Cet** étudiant travaille dans un restaurant.

DANS LA CUISINE
Say What You See

HERE'S WHAT WE CAME UP WITH:

Trois amis cuisinent ensemble dans une cuisine moderne. Ils ont chacun un verre de vin rouge devant eux. La première femme à gauche est blonde et porte une chemise. Au milieu, son amie aux cheveux bruns porte un tablier et fait sauter des légumes dans une poêle. Enfin, à droite un homme aux cheveux bruns porte une chemise à carreaux et regarde les légumes qui cuisent. Il y a plein d'aliments sur le plan de travail. On peut voir au premier plan un bol de citrons, un morceau de fromage et des radis frais.

TOUT OBJECTIF SANS PLAN N'EST QU'UN SOUHAIT
Guided Translation

TRANSLATION: "Every goal without a plan is only a wish".

PARTICIPES PRÉSENTS ET ADJECTIFS
Mini Grammar Challenge

I. J'ai trouvé ce concert **épatant** ! / Selon moi, / À mon avis, ce concert était **épatant** !

EXPLANATION:

- We can use the present participle of the verb **épater**
  as an adjective, meaning "impressive, amazing".

- While there are other ways you could adapt the structure of this sentence, some options are to add **j'ai trouvé, selon moi** or **à mon avis**. The important thing, however, is to use the adjective **épatant** to describe the noun **concert**.

2. Le bruit du trafic est si / tellement **assourdissant** que je ne vous entends pas. / Le bruit du trafic est **assourdissant**, à tel point que je ne vous entends pas. / Le bruit du trafic est **assourdissant**, donc je ne vous entends pas.

EXPLANATION: The adjective **assourdissant** ("deafening") is the present participle of the verb **assourdir**.

3. Paul est très **souriant** et ne semble jamais être de mauvaise humeur.

EXPLANATION: From the verb **sourire**, we get the present participle **souriant** ("smiling") and the adjective **souriant** ("smiley").

EN COURS
Say What You See

HERE'S WHAT WE CAME UP WITH:

Nous sommes dans une salle de classe, en cours de maths. L'institutrice est souriante, debout devant la classe. Derrière elle, il y a des calculs au tableau. Devant elle, les élèves assis à leurs bureaux sont sages et enthousiastes. Ils lèvent tous le doigt, car ils connaissent la réponse. L'institutrice choisit un élève pour répondre à sa question, et elle pointe du doigt un enfant au fond à gauche. Dans l'autre main, elle tient un grand cahier noir. Pour donner cours aujourd'hui, elle a mis un jean, une chemise blanche et un gilet.

APPRENDRE À UN VIEUX SINGE À FAIRE LA GRIMACE
Guided Translation

The literal translation of **ce n'est pas à un vieux singe qu'on apprend à faire la grimace** is "it's not to an old monkey that one teaches how to make faces" or "you don't teach an old monkey how to make faces".

Although this sounds similar to the English expression "you can't teach an old dog new tricks", it actually has a different meaning. It means that there is no substitute for experience. The idea is that you don't teach something to someone who has more experience in or more knowledge of the subject. An equivalent would be "you can't teach granny how to suck eggs".

Here are two examples of how this expression can be used:

Il essaie toujours de donner des conseils au plombier, mais ce n'est pas à un vieux singe qu'on apprend à faire la grimace.
He always tries to give the plumber advice, but you don't teach an expert how to do their job.

Je sais très bien que tu as mangé tout le chocolat. Ce n'est pas à un vieux singe qu'on apprend à faire la

grimace.

I know very well that you ate all the chocolate. I wasn't born yesterday.

We hope this has helped you to understand the proverb **ce n'est pas à un vieux singe qu'on apprend à faire la grimace.** In your next writing activity, have a go at writing your own example using this expression. **Bonne chance !**

OBJETS DU QUOTIDIEN
Word Builder

1. Je suis un robinet.
2. Je suis un congélateur.
3. Je suis un micro-ondes.
4. Je suis une poubelle.
5. Je suis un ordinateur.

PRONOMS RELATIFS
Mini Grammar Challenge

1. Paris est la ville **qu'**elle aime le plus.
2. La maison **que** nous allons acheter est près du supermarché.
3. La dame **qui** habite ici est très gentille.
4. Tu connais le chef **qui** travaille dans ce restaurant ?
5. Le film **qu'**on a vu l'autre jour était très intéressant.
6. Le rêve **que** j'ai fait hier soir était vraiment bizarre.
7. Il y a des fleurs **qui** poussent dans le jardin.
8. Le modèle **que** vous voulez n'est plus disponible.

9. Ce sont les voisins **qui** viennent dîner ce soir.
10. La ville **que** nous visitons est charmante.

AU CAFÉ
Say What You See

HERE'S WHAT WE CAME UP WITH:

Trois amis sont à la terrasse d'un café. Ils boivent un café en plein air car il fait beau. On peut voir derrière eux des arbres et des panneaux dans la rue. Sur leur table, il y a des tasses de café, une tablette et des lunettes. Au tout premier plan, il y a un petit bouquet de fleurs blanches. Les amis portent des vêtements légers. La dame assise au centre porte un t-shirt à rayures. Elle regarde son amie à sa gauche qui met sa main sur son épaule avec un grand sourire. Cette dame porte de grandes lunettes. À gauche de la photo, l'homme rit avec les filles, en se mettant la main sur les yeux. Il porte un chapeau noir.

LES ARBRES QUI GRANDISSENT LE PLUS LENTEMENT
Guided Translation

TRANSLATION: "The trees that are the slowest to grow are those that bear the best fruit".

Did you figure out why the word **meilleur** is used to mean "best", rather than **mieux**? Both words can be used as comparatives (**meilleur / mieux** - "better") and as superlatives (**le meilleur / le mieux** - "the best"). However, remember that **meilleur** is usually an adjective and so can be used with a noun, while **mieux** is an adverb and is therefore used with a verb. In our example, **meilleur** is being used to describe the noun **fruits** and so, like all adjectives, it must agree in gender and number, leaving us with **meilleurs** in the masculine plural form.

10-MINUTE COFFEE BREAKS

CHECKLIST
10-MINUTE COFFEE BREAKS

Translation Challenge

Famous French Speakers

Jumbled Letters

Number Focus

❏ Dates importantes - page 81

❏ L'accord des nombres - page 97

❏ Des prix - page 113

❏ À quelle heure ... ? - page 128

Taste Bud Tantaliser

❏ Salade niçoise - page 84

❏ Quatre-quarts - page 100

❏ Tapenade d'olives noires - page 115

❏ Gratin dauphinois - page 130

21

DÉFI DE TRADUCTION 1
TRANSLATION CHALLENGE

For this activity, we've given you some sentences in English to translate into French. Try them on your own first, then if you need some help, turn the page to find some hints. **Allez, on y va !**

* * *

1. I think it's going to rain. Don't forget to take an umbrella!

    ✎_____
    _____
    _____

2. Is the dessert included in today's menu?

    ✎_____
    _____
    _____

3. I wonder why they are not home yet.

    ✎_____

_____

_____

4. My son has a headache. Do you have a painkiller?

✎_____

_____

_____

5. There is no more milk in the fridge.

✎_____

_____

_____

HINTS

If you need some help, you may find the following hints useful.

1. In number 1, use the imperative.
2. In number 2, you can use the past participle of **inclure** ("to include"), which is **inclus**.
3. In number 3, use the present tense in the first part of the sentence and the perfect tense in the second part.
4. In the first sentence of number 4, think about the literal translation "my son has pain in the head".
5. In number 5, use the negative structure **ne ... plus**, which means "no more" or "no longer".

* * *

Once you're happy with your answers, have a look at our suggested translations on page 134.

22

CHARLES DE GAULLE
FAMOUS FRENCH SPEAKERS

This reading text is about an important figure in France's history: Charles de Gaulle. Use the vocabulary list on the next page to help you as you read through it, then answer the comprehension questions to test your understanding. **Bonne lecture !**

* * *

Charles de Gaulle, généralement connu sous le nom de "Général de Gaulle", était un homme politique et un dirigeant de l'armée durant quelques-unes des heures les plus critiques de la France. Il a servi en tant qu'officier durant la Première Guerre mondiale, puis est devenu chef de la Résistance contre l'Allemagne nazie durant la Deuxième Guerre mondiale. Il était le préféré des Français après la Libération. En 1958, il est intervenu dans la guerre d'Algérie, ancienne colonie française, et est devenu président de la République. Il est resté au pouvoir pendant plus de dix ans, jusqu'au changement social suivant les manifestations étudiantes de mai 68.

VOCABULARY

homme (m) **politique** - politician
dirigeant (m) - leader
critique - critical
servi < servir - served < to serve
en tant que - as
la Première Guerre (f) **mondiale** - the First World War
chef (m) - leader
la Résistance (f) - the Resistance
la Deuxième Guerre (f) **mondiale** - the Second World War
intervenu < intervenir - intervened < to intervene
ancien/ne - former
au pouvoir - in power
suivant < suivre - following < to follow
manifestation (f) - protest, demonstration

COMPREHENSION QUESTIONS

Answer the questions in English.

1. According to the text, during which period in France did Charles de Gaulle serve as a military leader?

_____

_____

2. What role did he play during: a) the First World War? b) the Second World War?

✎ _____

_____

3. How is Algeria described in the text?

✎ _____

_____

4. For how long did de Gaulle serve as President of France?

✎ _____

_____

5. What followed the period of unrest that began in May 1968?

✎ _____

_____

* * *

Once you've had a go, turn to page 137 to check your answers.

23

ANAGRAMME 1
JUMBLED LETTERS

In this activity you'll find two definitions and two words whose letters have been jumbled up. Your task is to unscramble the letters to find the word being defined. If you need some help, turn to page 80 to find a hint. Then, see how many other words in French (of three or more letters) you can make using the letters. **Bonne chance !**

* * *

I. DEFINITION: équipement qu'on utilise pour contrôler à distance un appareil, par exemple, une télévision.

MÉCDOLÉNTEMA

✎ _____   _____

_____   _____

_____   _____

_____   _____

_____   _____
_____   _____
_____   _____
_____   _____
_____   _____
_____   _____
_____

2. DEFINITION: d'une manière rapide et soudaine.

QTESURMUBNE

HINTS

1. This word is a feminine noun which is related to the verb **commander** ("to order, control").
2. This word is an adverb. Adverbs in French often end in -**ment**.

* * *

Once you've had a go, turn to page 138 to check your answers.

24

DATES IMPORTANTES
NUMBER FOCUS

Below, you will find a list of years and a list of events that took place across the French-speaking world over the last 500 years. First, write the dates as numerical figures. Then, have a go at writing each date below its corresponding event, listed on the next page. **C'est parti !**

* * *

LES DATES

1. deux mille un

   ✎ _____

2. mille sept cent quatre-vingt-neuf

   ✎ _____

3. mille neuf cent soixante-deux

   ✎ _____

4. deux mille

   ✎ _____

5. mille neuf cent soixante-dix

   ✎_____

6. mille huit cent trente-et-un

   ✎_____

7. mille neuf cent quinze

   ✎_____

8. mille cinq cent trente-quatre

   ✎_____

LES ÉVÈNEMENTS

1. La création de l'Organisation internationale de la Francophonie (OIF), qui représente des pays et des régions francophones partout dans le monde.

   ✎_____

2. La prise de la Bastille à Paris : moment devenu symbolique de la Révolution française.

   ✎_____

3. L'année de naissance de la chanteuse française Édith Piaf.

   ✎_____

4. Le premier voyage de l'explorateur français Jacques Cartier vers le territoire qui s'appelle actuellement la province du Québec.

   ✎_____

5. La Belgique et les Pays-Bas reçoivent l'Euro de football.

   ✎_____

6. La fin de la guerre d'Algérie, marquant

l'indépendance de l'Algérie de la France.

✎_____

7. La sortie du film *Le Fabuleux Destin d'Amélie Poulain*.

✎_____

8. L'intronisation du premier roi de la Belgique indépendante, Léopold Ier. Cette date est reconnue chaque année le 21 juillet, qui est la Fête nationale belge.

✎_____

* * *

Once you've had a go, turn to page 140 to check your answers.

25

SALADE NIÇOISE
TASTE BUD TANTALISER

Below is a recipe for a **salade niçoise**. Read it through as many times as you need to, using the vocabulary list to help you. Then, complete the exercises that follow to test your knowledge of the imperative in French. If you'd like to get to know all the vocabulary even better, why not try following this recipe for **salade niçoise** and make it yourself at home?

* * *

INGRÉDIENTS

- quelques feuilles de salade fraîche
- 1 poivron (de la couleur que vous désirez)
- 4 grosses tomates
- 4 œufs durs
- 1 poignée d'olives noires
- 1 boîte de thon
- quelques filets d'anchois

- 2 jeunes oignons
- huile d'olive
- vinaigre de vin rouge
- basilic frais

PRÉPARATION

1. Créez un lit de salade au fond de l'assiette.
2. Lavez et coupez le poivron en petits cubes.
3. Lavez et coupez les tomates en quartiers.
4. Ajoutez les œufs durs, les olives, le thon, les anchois, et les jeunes oignons en petits morceaux.
5. Versez-y la vinaigrette avec l'huile et le vinaigre.
6. Couronnez le tout avec les feuilles de basilic.
7. Dégustez !

VOCABULARY

feuille (f) - leaf
poivron (m) - bell pepper
œuf (m) **dur** - hard-boiled egg
poignée (f) - handful
thon (m) - tuna
anchois (m) - anchovy
jeune oignon (m) - spring onion
huile (f) - oil
basilic (m) - basil
au fond - at the bottom
versez < verser - pour < to pour
couronner - to crown
déguster - to taste, to enjoy

THE IMPERATIVE

Take a close look at the verbs in this recipe. They are all -**er** verbs that are conjugated in the **vous** form of the imperative, often known as "the command form". The imperative is used when you are telling or advising somebody to do something.

To form the **vous** form of the imperative, we simply take the **vous** form of the verb in the present tense and remove the subject pronoun (**vous**). For example:

regarder > **vous regardez** ("you look", present tense) > **regardez** ! ("look!", imperative)

The **tu** form of the imperative is formed by taking the **tu** form of the present tense and dropping the final -**s** of any conjugations that end in either -**es** or -**as**. We also remove the subject pronoun (**tu**).

regarder > **tu regardes** ("you look", present tense) > **regarde** ! ("look!", imperative)

There is an exception to this, however, which is when the verb is followed by the pronoun **y** or **en**. When this is the case, we keep the final -**s** in order to make the pronunciation smoother. Here's a very common example which you'll recognise: **vas-y** !

aller > **tu vas** > **va** ! > **vas-y** !

EXERCISE 1 - TRANSFORM

Now that we've reviewed how to form the imperative of -er verbs, imagine that you are making the salade niçoise with a friend or a child and, rather than reading the recipe, you are giving them these instructions directly. In this case, you would use the **tu** form of the imperative, rather than the **vous** form of the imperative. Fill in the gaps below, changing each conjugated verb into its **tu** form. Here's the first one to help you:

Crée [**créez**] un lit de salade au fond de l'assiette.

1. ✎_____ [**lavez**] et
   ✎_____ [**coupez**] le poivron en petits cubes.
2. ✎_____ [**ajoutez**] les œufs durs.
3. ✎_____ [**versez-y**] la vinaigrette.
4. ✎_____ [**couronnez**] le tout avec les feuilles de basilic.
5. ✎_____ [**dégustez**] !

EXERCISE 2 - IRREGULAR VERBS

While the vast majority of verbs follow the pattern we have just looked at, there are four verbs that are irregular in the imperative. Do you know which verbs the following imperative forms come from? For each sentence, give the infinitive of the verb being used, then try translating it.

1. **Sois** patient !

   INFINITIVE: ✎_____

   TRANSLATION: ✎_____

   _____

2. **N'ayez pas** peur de demander de l'aide.

   INFINITIVE: ✎_____

   TRANSLATION: ✎_____

   _____

3. **Sache** que tout va bien aller.

   INFINITIVE: ✎_____

   TRANSLATION: ✎_____

   _____

4. **Veuillez** vous asseoir.

   INFINITIVE: ✎_____

   TRANSLATION: ✎_____

   _____

* * *

When you're happy with your answers, turn to page 141 to check them.

26

DÉFI DE TRADUCTION 2
TRANSLATION CHALLENGE

Translate the following five sentences into French. Have a go on your own first, then if you need some help, turn the page to find a hint for each sentence. **Bonne chance !**

* * *

1. She went to the cinema yesterday evening.

   ✎_____

   _____

   _____

2. I am not going to eat any chocolate this week.

   ✎_____

   _____

   _____

3. When I was young, I used to play tennis every day.

   ✎_____

   _____

   _____

4. He was reading in the garden when his friends arrived.

✎_____

_____

_____

5. Before seeing the film, you must read the book.

✎_____

_____

_____

HINTS

If you need some help, you may find the following hints useful.

1. In sentence 1, use the perfect tense of the verb "to go" and think about which auxiliary verb to use.
2. In sentence 2, use the immediate future tense (**aller** in the present tense + infinitive).
3. In sentence 3, use the imperfect tense to describe this repeated action in the past.
4. Use the imperfect tense in the first part of sentence 4 and the perfect tense in the second part.
5. In sentence 5, use the verb **devoir**.

* * *

Once you've finished, turn to page 142 to take a look at our suggested translations.

27

MARIE CURIE
FAMOUS FRENCH SPEAKERS

This reading comprehension activity is based on a text about Marie Curie. Use the vocabulary list to help you with any unfamiliar words as you read through it, then answer the comprehension questions that follow. If you'd like an extra challenge, try reading the text and answering the questions before looking at the vocabulary list. Remember it's always there if you need some help!

* * *

Première femme à avoir obtenu un prix Nobel, et première à en avoir gagné deux, c'est une femme qui a inspiré des générations de femmes scientifiques. Nous parlons bien sûr de Marie Curie. Elle était d'origine polonaise mais est venue en France pour ses études, pour finalement y rester, devenir professeur à l'université de Paris et avancer dans ses recherches. Elle a découvert le radium, qui est un métal radioactif dangereux. Malheureusement, la cause de sa mort est bien connue car Marie Curie est décédée suite à une exposition trop forte à la radiation. Cependant, de nos jours, ses découvertes ont servi à tuer des cellules cancéreuses chez des patients malades.

VOCABULARY

obtenu < obtenir - received < to receive
en avoir gagné deux - to have won two of them
femme (f) **scientifique** - female scientist
d'origine polonaise - of Polish origin
y rester - to stay there
avancer - to move forward, to make progress
décédé/e < décéder - died < to die
suite à - following
exposition (f) - exposure
radiation (f) - radiation
de nos jours - nowadays
découverte (f) - discovery
ont servi à < servir - have been used to, have helped to < to serve
tuer - to kill
cellule (f) - cell
chez des patients malades - in sick patients

COMPREHENSION QUESTIONS

Answer the following questions in English.

1. How many times did Marie Curie win the Nobel Prize?

   ✎_____

   _____

2. Where did she spend the second part of her life?

   ✎_____

   _____

3. According to the text, what is well known about Marie Curie?

   ✎_____

   _____

4. How did she die?

   ✎_____

   _____

5. According to the text, in what way has she influenced today's medical practice?

   ✎_____

   _____

* * *

Super travail ! The answers can be found on page 144.

28

ANAGRAMME 2
JUMBLED LETTERS

In this anagram challenge, your task is to unscramble the letters of each of the two anagrams to find the word being described in the definition. If you need some help, turn to page 96 to find a hint for each anagram. Then, see how many other words in French (of three or more letters) you can make using the letters.

* * *

I. DEFINITION: penser pendant un certain temps, considérer.

HÉRCLRIFÉ

✎ _____ _____

_____ _____

_____ _____

_____ _____

_____ _____

_____   _____
_____   _____
_____   _____
_____   _____
_____   _____
_____

2. DEFINITION: manteau qu'on porte sous la pluie pour rester au sec.

PRELÉMIBAEM

_____   _____
_____   _____
_____   _____
_____   _____
_____   _____
_____   _____
_____   _____
_____   _____
_____   _____
_____

HINTS

1. The word you're looking for is a verb. All verbs in French end in either **-er**, **-ir** or **-re**. Check which of these combinations can be made using these letters to give you the ending of this word.
2. In informal, colloquial French, we often use an abbreviation of this word.

* * *

Très bien ! Once you've had a go, turn to page 145 to check your answers.

29

L'ACCORD DES NOMBRES
NUMBER FOCUS

In this Number Focus, we're taking a close look at a very specific aspect of numbers in French: the agreement of the number "one". Read the explanation below before having a go at the exercise.

* * *

For numbers ending in "one", the number "one" has to agree with the noun: **un** for masculine nouns and **une** for feminine nouns. For example:

un jour > vingt-et-un jours
one day > twenty-one days

The number **vingt-et-un** agrees with the noun **jour**, which is a masculine noun.

une semaine > vingt-et-une semaines
one week > twenty-one weeks

Here, the number **vingt-et-une** agrees with the noun **semaine**, which is a feminine noun.

EXERCISE

Translate the following phrases into French. Write the numbers out in words and make sure to pay attention to the gender of the noun.

1. 301 apples
   ✎_____

   _____

2. 561 bananas
   ✎_____

   _____

3. 231 cakes
   ✎_____

   _____

4. 481 birds
   ✎_____

   _____

5. 641 books
   ✎_____

   _____

6. 151 bottles
   ✎_____

   _____

7. 721 houses

 ✎___ _____

 _____

8. 861 euros

 ✎_____

 _____

9. 931 dollars

 ✎_____

 _____

10. 1001 stories

 ✎_____

 _____

* * *

Excellent travail ! Once you're ready, you can find the answers on page 147.

30

QUATRE-QUARTS
TASTE BUD TANTALISER

The **quatre-quarts**, otherwise known as a pound cake, is an easily prepared snack or dessert from the Brittany region of France. As its name suggests, it is made with an equal quantity (traditionally, 1 pound in weight) of each of the four main ingredients. Use the vocabulary list provided to help you read through this recipe for **quatre-quarts**, then answer the questions that follow to test your understanding.

* * *

INGRÉDIENTS

- 250 grammes de beurre
- 250 grammes de farine
- 250 grammes de sucre
- 4 œufs
- 1 sachet de levure
- quelques gouttes d'arôme de vanille

PRÉPARATION

1. Préchauffez le four à 180°C.
2. Faites fondre le beurre au bain-marie.
3. Ajoutez tous les ingrédients dans un saladier en mélangeant bien à chaque ajout.
4. Beurrez un moule et versez-y tout le mélange.
5. Laissez cuire pendant 45 minutes.
6. Après la cuisson, vérifiez que c'est cuit en plantant un couteau. Si le couteau est sec, à table !

VOCABULARY

quart (m) - quarter
farine (f) - flour
sachet (m) - packet
levure (f) - yeast
goutte (f) - drop
préchauffez < préchauffer - preheat < to preheat
fondre - to melt
ajouter - to add
saladier (m) - salad bowl
en mélangeant < mélanger - mixing < to mix
ajout (m) - addition
beurrer - to butter, to grease
moule (m) - baking tin, baking pan
cuisson (f) - baking, cooking process
cuit < cuire - cooked < to cook
en plantant < planter - by sticking, sinking < to stick, to sink
couteau (m) - knife
sec / sèche - dry

EXERCISE 1 - COMPREHENSION

Put the following instructions into the correct order, so that they match the directions given in the recipe.

a) Mix all the ingredients in a bowl.
b) Leave it to cook.
c) Preheat the oven.
d) Pour the mix into the greased baking tin.
e) Sink a knife into the cake to check it's cooked.
f) Melt the butter.

✎_____

EXERCISE 2 - FIND THE FRENCH

Now, find the French for the following phrases in the text. Note that they don't appear in the order given below.

1. it's cooked
   ✎_____

2. a few drops
   ✎_____

3. melt the butter
   ✎_____

4. with each addition
   ✎_____

5. preheat the oven
   ✎_____

6. all of the mix

✎_____

* * *

Once you've finished the exercises, turn to page 147 to check
your answers.

31

DÉFI DE TRADUCTION 3
TRANSLATION CHALLENGE

In this Translation Challenge, you have some sentences in English to translate into French. If you need some help, you can find a hint for each translation on the following page.

* * *

1. Do you want some bread? I've just bought some.

   ✎_____

   _____

   _____

2. I'm not going to go into town today. I went there yesterday.

   ✎_____

   _____

   _____

3. After reading the newspaper, she drank her coffee.

   ✎_____

_____

_____

4. Our aunt lives in an old house with a white door.

✎_____

_____

_____

5. We bought some croissants this morning. There are three of them.

✎_____

_____

_____

HINTS

If you need some help, you may find the following hints useful.

1. In the second sentence of number 1, use the construction **venir de** and the pronoun **en**.
2. Use the immediate future in the first sentence of number 2 and the perfect tense in the second one. You will also need the pronoun y to translate "there".
3. For number 3, begin your sentence with **après avoir**.
4. For number 4, think about where to place the adjectives in relation to the nouns.
5. In number 5, use the perfect tense and the pronoun **en**.

* * *

Très bon travail ! Once you're happy with your translations, turn to page 148 to find our suggested answers.

32

LOUIS PASTEUR
FAMOUS FRENCH SPEAKERS

The text below is all about Louis Pasteur. Read the text, use the vocabulary list on the next page to help you with any tricky vocabulary, and answer the questions that follow to test your understanding. **C'est parti !**

$$* * *$$

Louis Pasteur était un microbiologiste et chimiste français du 19ᵉ siècle. Il est reconnu pour ses recherches qui ont fait avancer la théorie du microbe. En effet, il a affirmé que les microbes pouvaient provoquer un grand nombre de maladies. C'est à lui qu'on doit l'existence des vaccins, notamment le vaccin contre la rage. Son nom de famille peut nous faire penser au verb "pasteuriser", et ce n'est pas un hasard. C'est Pasteur qui a trouvé le moyen de garder le lait bon à consommer pendant plus longtemps grâce à sa méthode de pasteurisation, en tuant les micro-organismes néfastes.

VOCABULARY

microbiologiste (m/f) - microbiologist

chimiste (m/f) - chemist

reconnu/e - recognised, famous

la théorie du microbe - germ theory

affirmé < affirmer - claimed < to claim

provoquer - to provoke, to cause

maladie (f) - illness, disease

c'est à lui qu'on doit - it's to him that we owe

vaccin (m) - vaccine

notamment - in particular

la rage - rabies

peut nous faire penser à - can make us think of

pasteuriser - to pasteurise

hasard (m) - chance, coincidence

en tuant < tuer - by killing < to kill

micro-organisme (m) - microorganism

néfaste - harmful

COMPREHENSION QUESTIONS

Answer the following questions in English.

1. According to the text, what did Louis Pasteur discover in his research?

   ✎ _____

   _____

2. Pasteur is responsible for the existence of which medical procedure?

✎_____

_____

3. The name of which disease is mentioned in the text?

✎_____

_____

4. What is said about his surname?

✎_____

_____

5. True or false: although Louis Pasteur named the process of pasteurisation, he was not responsible for its creation.

✎_____

_____

* * *

Once you're happy with your answers, turn to page 150 to check them.

33

ANAGRAMME 3
JUMBLED LETTERS

Unscramble the letters of each anagram below to find the word being defined. There is a hint for each anagram on the following page, if you need some help. Your second challenge is to find as many French words as you can (of three or more letters) using those letters. **Bonne chance !**

* * *

I. DEFINITION: qui évite de faire du travail, n'a pas envie de faire d'effort.

XASPERUSE

✎ _____   _____

_____   _____

_____   _____

_____   _____

_____   _____

_____   _____

_____   _____

_____   _____

_____   _____

_____   _____

_____

2. DEFINITION: insecte qui a quatre ailes colorées.

NLAPOLPI

_____   _____

_____   _____

_____   _____

_____   _____

_____   _____

_____   _____

_____   _____

_____   _____

_____   _____

_____

HINTS

1. The word you're looking for is an adjective, but it can also be a noun. Here, it is in its masculine form, but its feminine form would end in **-euse**.
2. This masculine noun contains a double l.

* * *

Once you've had a go, turn to page 151 to find the answers.

34

DES PRIX
NUMBER FOCUS

Knowing your numbers is important when it comes to handling money and prices in French. Let's practise this by re-writing the following sentences, writing the numbers out in words. **Allons-y !**

* * *

1. Les chaussures coûtent 92 €.

   ✎_____

   _____

2. Je voudrais retirer 250 €.

   ✎_____

   _____

3. Cette chemise coûte 79 €.

   ✎_____

   _____

4. Je voudrais changer 325 $ en francs suisses.

✎_____

_____

5. Ce manteau coûte 118 €.

✎_____

_____

6. Je voudrais changer 567 £ en euros.

✎_____

_____

7. Les billets sont à 44 €.

✎_____

_____

8. Le taxi coûte 36 €.

✎_____

_____

9. Je voudrais changer 403 € en livres.

✎_____

_____

10. Ça fait 81 € en tout.

✎_____

_____

* * *

Once you've had a go, turn to page 152 to check your answers.

35

TAPENADE D'OLIVES NOIRES
TASTE BUD TANTALISER

Read the recipe below and use the vocabulary list provided to help you with any unfamiliar words. Then, complete the language exercise that follows. Later, why not try making a **tapenade d'olives noires** yourself, to help you get to know all this new vocabulary?

* * *

INGRÉDIENTS

- 300 grammes d'olives noires dénoyautées
- 2 gousses d'ail
- 80 grammes de câpres
- 5 à 10 filets d'anchois dans de l'huile
- 1 cuillère à café d'origan
- 1 pincée de poivre
- 100 ml d'huile d'olive

PRÉPARATION

1. Mettez tous les ingrédients sauf l'huile d'olive dans un bon mixeur.
2. Commencez à mixer avec quelques pulsions.
3. Rajoutez progressivement l'huile d'olive.
4. Mixez jusqu'à obtenir la consistance souhaitée.

VOCABULARY

dénoyauté/e - pitted
gousse (f) - clove
ail (m) - garlic
câpre (m) - caper
filet (m) **d'anchois** (m) - anchovy fillet
huile (f) - oil
cuillère (f) **à café** - teaspoon, teaspoonful
origan (m) - oregano
pincée (f) - pinch
poivre (m) - pepper
sauf - except
mixeur (m) - mixer, blender
rajoutez < **rajouter** - add < to add
consistance (f) - consistency
souhaité/e - desired

LANGUAGE EXERCISE

Below are some words taken from the recipe. Complete the following sentences using the most appropriate word to fill each gap.

**dénoyautées | huile | cuillère | pincée | poivre |
sauf | progressivement | jusqu'à | obtenir | souhaitée**

1. Il y a beaucoup trop de ✎_____
   dans cette soupe et je n'aime pas la nourriture
   épicée !
2. J'aime bien les cerises, mais je préfère les acheter
   déjà ✎_____ .
3. Hélène a marché ✎_____ la
   plage, mais quand il a commencé à pleuvoir elle a
   décidé de rentrer chez elle.
4. Maman m'a toujours dit de ne pas ajouter plus d'une
   ✎_____ de sel dans un plat,
   parce que ce n'est pas bon pour la santé.
5. Heureusement, le réparateur de vélo m'a dit que la
   chaîne de vélo fonctionnait bien et qu'elle avait tout
   simplement besoin d'un peu
   d'✎_____ .
6. Maintenant que j'habite à Madrid, j'améliore
   ✎_____ mon espagnol en
   parlant avec mes nouveaux voisins et avec les gens
   qui travaillent dans l'épicerie du coin.
7. Mélanie, tu prends une seule

✎_____ de sucre dans ton thé
ou plus ?

8. À chaque fois que j'essaie de faire des croissants à la
maison, ils n'ont jamais la forme
✎_____ , mais ils sont délicieux
quand même !

9. Tous les invités sont arrivés à l'heure,
✎_____ Jean qui a manqué son
train et qui est donc arrivé avec une demi-heure de
retard.

10. Vous pensez qu'il serait possible
d'✎_____ ce livre avant lundi
prochain ? J'en ai vraiment besoin.

* * *

Bravo ! When you've finished, turn to page 153 to find the
answers.

36

DÉFI DE TRADUCTION 4
TRANSLATION CHALLENGE

Below are some sentences to translate into French. Have a go without any help first, then take a look at the hints on the next page if you need to.

* * *

1. Anne went for a walk with her sister.

   ✎_____

   _____

   _____

2. Did you see this film? It's great!

   ✎_____

   _____

   _____

3. I'm hungry. Let's go to the restaurant.

   ✎_____

   _____

   _____

4. The neighbours visited us on Monday evening.

    ✎ _____

    _____

    _____

5. My parents met when they were seventeen.

    ✎ _____

    _____

    _____

HINTS

If you need some help, you may find the following hints useful.

1. In number 1, the reflexive verb **se promener** can be used to translate "to go for a walk". Think carefully about which auxiliary verb reflexive verbs take in a compound tense, such as the perfect tense.

2. For number 2, think carefully about which tense to use.

3. For number 3, remember that in French we literally say "I have hunger", rather than "I am hungry".

4. For number 4, think carefully about how to translate "to visit somebody". You will also need to use the indirect object pronoun **nous** in this sentence.

5. In number 5, you will need to use the reflexive verb **se rencontrer**. Like in number 1, think carefully about the auxiliary verb you're going to use to construct the perfect tense.

* * *

Bravo ! Now, turn to page 154 to read our suggested translations.

37

AMÉLIE MAURESMO
FAMOUS FRENCH SPEAKERS

The following text is about former tennis player Amélie Mauresmo. Try noting down any new vocabulary as you read through the text to help you remember it. Then, answer the comprehension questions that follow.

* * *

Née en 1979 à Saint-Germain-en-Laye, Amélie Mauresmo était une joueuse de tennis professionnelle. Passionnée par ce sport depuis l'âge de quatre ans, et après s'être montrée extrêmement talentueuse pendant sa jeunesse, elle est arrivée en finale de l'Australian Open de 1999. En 2004, elle a été vice-championne olympique à Athènes. C'est à cette période qu'elle est devenue la première joueuse française de l'ère moderne à atteindre le classement de numéro 1 mondial, et la seconde dans toute l'histoire du tennis féminin.

VOCABULARY

passionné/e par - passionate about

depuis - since

après s'être montrée - after having shown herself to be

talentueux/euse - talented

période (f) - time, stage

ère (f) - era, age

atteindre - to reach

classement (m) - ranking

tennis (m) **féminin** - women's tennis

COMPREHENSION QUESTIONS

Answer the questions in English.

1. When did Amélie Mauresmo first become interested in tennis?

   ✎ _____

   _____

2. True or false: Mauresmo's interest and success in tennis were inconsistent throughout her youth.

   ✎ _____

   _____

3. What happened in 1999?

   ✎ _____

   _____

4. Mauresmo became the first French female tennis player to do what?

   ✎ _____

   _____

5. Mauresmo became the second French female tennis player to do what?

✎ _____

_____

* * *

Excellent travail ! You can check your answers on page 157.

38

ANAGRAMME 4
JUMBLED LETTERS

In this activity, your task is to unscramble the letters of each anagram below to find the word being defined. If you need some help, turn to page 127 to find a hint. Then, see how many words in French (of three or more letters) you can make using the letters of the anagram.

* * *

I. DEFINITION: concernant un avion, toucher le sol en arrivant à sa destination.

RTIRARTE

✎_____   _____

_____   _____

_____   _____

_____   _____

_____   _____

_____   _____
_____   _____
_____   _____
_____   _____
_____   _____
_____

2. DEFINITION: avec plaisir, de bonne volonté.

STONVEROIL

_____   _____
_____   _____
_____   _____
_____   _____
_____   _____
_____   _____
_____   _____
_____   _____
_____   _____
_____

HINTS

1. The word you're looking for is a verb which contains a double t and a double r.
2. This is an adverb that is very often used as a single word on its own: for example, to respond to an invitation or a request that you want to accept.

* * *

Très bon travail ! The anagram solutions can be found on page 157.

39

À QUELLE HEURE … ?
NUMBER FOCUS

In this activity, we're going to practise our numbers in the context of time. In French, the 24-hour clock is used when talking about the time. Replace the phrases in brackets with the correct French translation.

Here's an example to help you:

> Il quitte le travail à [6pm].
> *Il quitte le travail à dix-huit heures.*

* * *

1. Je rentre à la maison à [7pm].

   ✎_____

   _____

2. Nous dînons ensemble à [8pm].

   ✎_____

   _____

3. La fête commence à [9pm].

   ✎_____

   _____

4. Mes collègues déjeunent à [1pm].

   ✎_____

   _____

5. Les enfants prennent le goûter à [4pm].

   ✎_____

   _____

6. Le cours se termine à [5pm].

   ✎_____

   _____

7. On va voir un film à [3pm].

   ✎_____

   _____

8. Vous avez un rendez-vous à [2pm].

   ✎_____

   _____

9. Le train arrive à [11pm].

   ✎_____

   _____

10. Je vais me coucher à [10pm].

    ✎_____

    _____

* * *

Once you're happy with your answers, turn to page 160 to check them.

40

GRATIN DAUPHINOIS
TASTE BUD TANTALISER

The **gratin dauphinois** is a classic French dish which is easy to find in most traditional restaurants in the country. It's also a hearty meal that's easy to make at home, especially when you have many mouths to feed. Read the recipe for **gratin dauphinois,** then have a go at the exercises that follow. If you'd like an extra challenge, try reading the text and completing the exercises before looking at the vocabulary list. **Allons-y !**

* * *

INGRÉDIENTS

- 6 grosses pommes de terre
- 80 centilitres de crème fraîche
- de la noix de muscade
- du sel et du poivre
- du gruyère râpé

PRÉPARATION

1. Coupez les pommes de terre en fines lamelles.
2. Disposez les lamelles au fond du plat.
3. Couvrez d'un lit de crème fraîche.
4. Ajoutez les aromates.
5. Répétez l'opération, en ajoutant les couches de pommes de terre et la crème à chaque fois.
6. Quand le plat est rempli, saupoudrez le tout avec le gruyère.
7. Enfournez pendant 50 minutes à 180°C.

VOCABULARY

noix de muscade (f) - nutmeg
râpé/e - grated
coupez < couper - cut, slice < to cut, to slice
fin/e - thin
lamelle (f) - slice
au fond (m) - at the bottom
plat (m) - dish
couvrir - to cover
lit (m) - bed
aromates (m, pl) - spices, seasoning
couche (f) - layer
rempli/e - full
saupoudrer - to sprinkle
enfourner - to put in the oven

EXERCISE 1 - COMPREHENSION

Are the following statements true or false, **vrai ou faux?** Circle your answer for each statement, and if false, give the correct statement.

1. The first step is to mix the seasoning. VRAI | FAUX

   ✎ _____

   _____

2. The potatoes should be cut into bite-sized chunks. VRAI | FAUX

   ✎ _____

   _____

3. A layer of crème fraîche goes on top of each layer of potato. VRAI | FAUX

   ✎ _____

   _____

4. A layer of cheese is then spread over each layer of crème fraîche. VRAI | FAUX

   ✎ _____

   _____

5. The dish is cooked for less than one hour. VRAI | FAUX

   ✎ _____

   _____

EXERCISE 2 - FIND THE FRENCH

Now, find the French for the following phrases in the text. Note that they don't appear in the order given below.

1. each time

   🖊_____

2. the dish is full

   🖊_____

3. arrange the slices

   🖊_____

4. grated gruyère cheese

   🖊_____

5. in thin slices

   🖊_____

* * *

Once you've had a go, turn to page 160 to check your answers.

ANSWERS
10-MINUTE COFFEE BREAKS

DÉFI DE TRADUCTION 1
Translation Challenge

1. Je pense qu'il va pleuvoir. N'oublie pas / N'oubliez pas de prendre un parapluie !

EXPLANATION:

- In French, we need to say "I think *that* ...", so the verb **penser** has to be followed by **que**.
- The immediate future is formed of the present tense of the verb **aller** followed by an infinitive.
- The imperative is used when giving someone advice or telling someone to do something. It's not clear whether this situation is formal or informal, so either **oublie** or **oubliez** can be used.
- The negative is formed by putting **ne** and **pas** around

the conjugated verb. Since the verb begins with a
vowel, the **ne** becomes **n'**.
- "To bring", in the sense of bringing something
somewhere, would usually be **apporter**. Here,
however, we are talking about bringing something
along, which would be better translated using
prendre.

2. Est-ce que le dessert est inclus dans le menu du jour ?

EXPLANATION:

- Remember that there are various ways of asking
questions in French. We have used **est-ce que** above,
which means that we don't have to use inversion. If you
chose the inverted question form, however, this would
be **le dessert est-il inclus dans le menu du jour ?**
Alternatively, we can just add a question mark to the
statement **le dessert est inclus dans le menu du jour ?**
- **Un menu du jour** ("a daily / set menu") is found in
most restaurants, even in more informal snack bars.
- **Inclus** is the past participle of the verb **inclure**.

3. Je me demande pourquoi ils ne sont pas encore rentrés /
elles ne sont pas encore rentrées.

EXPLANATION:

- "To wonder" can be translated using the reflexive

verb **se demander**, which literally means "to ask oneself".

- In the perfect tense, the adverb **encore** is placed between the auxiliary verb and the past participle.
- To form the negative of the perfect tense, we place **ne** and **pas** around the conjugated verb, which is the auxiliary verb.
- The verb **rentrer**, meaning "to come back", is very commonly used to refer specifically to the idea of returning home. You could elaborate by saying **rentré(e)s à la maison**, but **rentrer** on its own is enough in this context.
- **Rentrer** takes **être** as the auxiliary verb in the perfect tense. This means that the past participle has to agree with the subject. Since the subject is plural, an extra **-s** is added to the past participle. If "they" refers to a group of all females, an extra **-es** is added to the past participle in the sentence **elles ne sont pas encore rentrées.**

4. Mon fils a mal à la tête. Est-ce que tu as / vous avez un anti-douleur ?

EXPLANATION:

- You can also use the construction **avoir un mal de tête** ("to have a headache"). In this context, this would give us **mon fils a un mal de tête.**
- To form the question, we can either use **est-ce que**, as above, use the inverted form of the verb (**as-tu /**

avez-vous un antidouleur ?), or simply say **tu as /
vous avez un antidouleur ?**, with a question mark at
the end.

- **Un antidouleur** is the word for "a painkiller" and
literally means "anti-pain".

5. Il n'y a plus de lait dans le frigo.

EXPLANATION:

- If we wanted to say "there is no milk", this would be
il n'y a pas de lait. But in order to say "there is no
more milk", **pas** must be replaced by **plus**.
- In the negative, the partitive articles **du, de la** and **de
l'** are replaced by **de** or **d'**. **Du lait** ("some milk")
therefore becomes **pas de lait** ("no milk") or **plus de
lait** ("no more milk"). Remember that the -s on the
end of **plus** is not pronounced in a negative context.
- Also pay attention to the position of the negative
particles **ne** and **plus**. **Plus** comes after the
conjugated verb: in this case, **a** from **avoir**. Here, **ne**
is followed by a vowel (**y**), so it becomes **n'**.

CHARLES DE GAULLE
Famous French Speakers

1. During one of the most critical eras in France.
2. a) He served as an officer.
b) He was the leader of the French Resistance against
Nazi Germany.

3. A former French colony.
4. For more than ten years.
5. Social change.

ANAGRAMME 1
Jumbled Letters

1. **télécommande** (f) - remote control

While there are many words that can be made out of these letters, here are some of the most common ones:

- **clé** (f) - key
- **mal** (m) - bad
- **mal** - badly
- **mec** (m) - guy
- **met** (from **mettre**) - puts
- **mot** (m) - word
- **nom** (m) - name
- **cela** - that, this
- **cent** (m) - hundred
- **dame** (f) - woman
- **date** (f) - date
- **donc** - therefore
- **dont** - whose, of which
- **lent** - slow
- **ment** (from **mentir**) - lies
- **télé** (f) - TV
- **admet** (from **admettre**) - admits
- **amené** (from **amener**) - brought

- **calme** (m) - calm
- **comme** - like
- **conte** (f) - story
- **lance** (from **lancer**) - throw(s)
- **monde** (m) - world
- **monte / monté** (from **monter**) - ascend(s) / ascended
- **oncle** (m) - uncle
- **moment** (m) - moment
- **comment** - how
- **élément** (m) - element
- **commande** (f) - order
- **commandé** (from **commander**) - controlled

2. **brusquement** - suddenly, abruptly

- **but** (m) - goal, aim
- **est** (from **être**) - is
- **mer** (f) - sea
- **met** (from **mettre**) - puts
- **nu/e** - naked, bare
- **rue** (f) - street
- **brun** - brown
- **mens / ment** (from **mentir**) - lie(s)
- **muet** - silent, mute
- **sent** (from **sentir**) - smells, feels
- **sert** (from **servir**) - serves
- **tuer** - to kill
- **brume** (f) - mist
- **entre / entres** (from **entrer**) - enter(s)
- **mener** - to lead

- **meurs / meurt** (from **mourir**) - die(s)
- **queue** (f) - tail, queue
- **reste** (from **rester**) - stay(s), remain(s)
- **Serbe** (m/f) - Serb
- **serbe** - Serbian
- **sueur** (f) - sweat
- **tenue** (f) - outfit
- **terme** (m) - term, limit
- **mesure** (f) - amount, measure
- **Turque** (f) - Turkish woman
- **turque** - Turkish
- **menteur** (m) - liar
- **brusquent** (from **brusquer**) - rush

DATES IMPORTANTES
Number Focus

LES DATES:

1. 2001
2. 1789
3. 1962
4. 2000
5. 1970
6. 1831
7. 1915
8. 1534

LES ÉVÈNEMENTS:

1. 1970
2. 1789
3. 1915
4. 1534
5. 2000
6. 1962
7. 2001
8. 1831

SALADE NIÇOISE
Taste Bud Tantaliser

EXERCISE 1 - TRANSFORM

1. **Lave** et **coupe** le poivron en petits cubes.
2. **Ajoute** les œufs durs.
3. **Verses-y** la vinaigrette.
4. **Couronne** le tout avec les feuilles de basilic.
5. **Déguste** !

EXERCISE 2 - IRREGULAR VERBS

1. INFINITIVE: **être. Sois** is the **tu** form of the imperative of the verb **être** ("to be").
   TRANSLATION: *Be patient!*
2. INFINITIVE: **avoir. Ayez** is the **vous** form of the imperative of the verb **avoir** ("to have"). Here, it is

used as a negative command.

TRANSLATION: *Don't be afraid to ask for help.*

3. INFINITIVE: **savoir. Sache** is the **tu** form of the imperative of the verb **savoir** ("to know").

TRANSLATION: *Know that everything is going to be ok.*

4. INFINITIVE: **vouloir. Veuillez** is the **vous** form of the imperative of the verb **vouloir** ("to want"). It is an interesting example, as when **vouloir** is used in the imperative, it adds an element of politeness to a request or an order. It can generally be thought of as an equivalent of **s'il vous plaît**.

TRANSLATION: *Please sit down.*

DÉFI DE TRADUCTION 2
Translation Challenge

1. Elle est allée au cinéma hier soir.

EXPLANATION:

- The verb **aller** takes the auxiliary verb **être** in the perfect tense. This means that the past participle has to agree with the subject. Since the subject is feminine, we add an extra **-e** to the end of the past participle.
- When you combine **à** with the masculine definite article (**le**), **à** + **le** becomes **au**.

2. Je ne vais pas manger de chocolat cette semaine.

EXPLANATION:

- The immediate future is formed of the present tense of the verb **aller**, followed by an infinitive.
- To form the negative of the immediate future, we put **ne** and **pas** around the conjugated verb.
- In the negative, **du**, **de la** and **de l'** are replaced by **de** or **d'**.
- When the noun is feminine, for example **semaine** ("week"), the word for "this" is **cette**.

3. Quand j'étais jeune, je jouais au tennis tous les jours.

EXPLANATION:

- The imperfect tense is used when talking about a habitual or an ongoing action in the past.
- Since **jours** is a masculine plural noun, the masculine plural form of **tous** is used.

4. Il lisait dans le jardin quand ses amis sont arrivés / ses amies sont arrivées.

EXPLANATION:

- The imperfect tense is used in the first part of the sentence to talk about an ongoing action.
- The perfect tense is used in the second part of the

sentence to talk about an action that interrupted an ongoing activity.

- The verb **arriver** takes **être** as the auxiliary verb. This means that the past participle has to agree with the subject. Since the subject is plural, an extra **-s** is added to the past participle. If the friends were all female, we would also add an extra **-e**, giving us **arrivées**.

5. Avant de voir le film, tu dois lire le livre / vous devez lire le livre.

EXPLANATION:

- When the subject is the same in both parts of the sentence, we use the **avant de** + infinitive construction to say "before doing something".
- The verb **devoir** + infinitive is used to say "must do something" in French.

MARIE CURIE
Famous French Speakers

1. Twice.
2. In France.
3. The cause of her death.
4. She died following high levels of radiation exposure.
5. Her discoveries have been used to kill cancer cells in sick patients.

ANAGRAMME 2
Jumbled Letters

1. **réfléchir** - to think, to reflect

Here are some of the common words that can be made out of these letters:

- **cil** (m) - eyelash
- **clé** (f) - key
- **cri** (m) - shout, cry
- **fil** (m) - thread
- **hic** (m) - hiccup, problem
- **crié / crier** - shouted / to shout
- **flic** (m) - cop, police officer
- **fric** (m) - money
- **chéri** (m) - darling, beloved

2. **imperméable** (m) - raincoat

- **ail** (m) - garlic
- **air** (m) - air, appearance
- **ami/e** (m/f) - friend
- **bar** (m) - bar
- **bel** - beautiful
- **ira** (from **aller**) - will go
- **mai** - May
- **mal** (m) - bad
- **mal** - badly
- **mer** (f) - sea

- **par** - by, through
- **abri** (m) - shelter
- **aile** (f) - wing
- **arme** (f) - weapon
- **baie** (f) - bay, berry
- **bail** (m) - lease, a long time
- **brie** (m) - brie
- **lire** - to read
- **miel** (m) - honey
- **pile** (f) - battery
- **pile** - on the dot
- **pire** (m) - the worst
- **pire** - worse
- **aimer** - to love
- **email** (m) - email
- **imper** (m) (abbreviation of **imperméable**) - raincoat
- **lampe** (f) - lamp
- **libre** - free
- **maire** (m/f) - mayor
- **marié** (from **marier**) - married
- **parle / parlé** (from **parler**) - speak(s) / spoke
- **parmi** - among
- **pareil** - the same
- **plaire** - to please
- **rempli/e** - full

L'ACCORD DES NOMBRES
Number Focus

1. trois-cent-une pommes
2. cinq-cent-soixante-et-une bananes
3. deux-cent-trente-et-un gâteaux
4. quatre-cent-quatre-vingt-un oiseaux
5. six-cent-quarante-et-un livres
6. cent cinquante-et-une bouteilles
7. sept-cent-vingt-et-une maisons
8. huit-cent-soixante-et-un euros
9. neuf-cent-trente-et-un dollars
10. mille-et-une histoires

QUATRE-QUARTS
Taste Bud Tantaliser

EXERCISE I - COMPREHENSION

c), f), a), d), b), e)

EXERCISE 2 - FIND THE FRENCH

1. c'est cuit
2. quelques gouttes
3. faites fondre le beurre
4. à chaque ajout
5. préchauffez le four
6. tout le mélange

DÉFI DE TRADUCTION 3
Translation Challenge

1. Tu veux / Vous voulez du pain ? Je viens d'en acheter.

EXPLANATION:

- You could also say **veux-tu du pain ? / voulez-vous du pain ?** or **est-ce que tu veux du pain ? / est-ce que vous voulez du pain ?**
- The partitive articles **du, de la** and **de l'** are used to talk about an unspecified amount of something. As **pain** is a masculine singular noun, we use **du**.
- The **venir de** + infinitive construction is used to mean "to have just done something".
- The pronoun **en** refers back to **du pain** and, here, it can be thought of as meaning "some of it". In situations where you have two verbs, such as **venir de** + infinitive, **en** is placed just before the infinitive.

2. Je ne vais pas aller en ville aujourd'hui. J'y suis allé/e hier.

EXPLANATION:

- The immediate future is formed of the present tense of the verb **aller**, followed by an infinitive.
- To form the negative of the immediate future, we place **ne** and **pas** around the conjugated verb.
- The pronoun **y** almost always comes before the verb. In the perfect tense, **y** comes before the

auxiliary verb and the past participle. When **je** is
followed by a vowel, we shorten it to **j'**, so here it
becomes **j'y**.

- The verb **aller** takes the auxiliary verb **être**. This
  means that the past participle has to agree with the
  subject. If the subject is feminine, an extra -**e** is
  added to the past participle.

3. Après avoir lu le journal, elle a bu son café.

EXPLANATION:

- The **après avoir** + past participle construction is
  used to mean "after having done something".
- Possessive adjectives must agree in gender and
  number with the noun they refer to. Therefore, **son**
  agrees with **café**, which is a masculine singular
  noun.

4. Notre tante habite dans une vieille maison avec une porte
blanche.

EXPLANATION:

- In French, adjectives have to agree in gender and
  number with the noun they are describing. Since
  maison and **porte** are both feminine nouns, the
  adjectives **vieille** and **blanche** are in their feminine
  form.
- The adjective **vieille** is an example of an adjective

that comes before the noun it is describing, whereas **blanche** comes after the noun.

5. Nous avons acheté / On a acheté des croissants ce matin. Il y en a trois.

EXPLANATION:

- When the noun is masculine and begins with a consonant, for example **matin** ("morning"), the word for "this" is **ce**.
- Here, the pronoun **en** stands for "of them" and is placed before the verb.

LOUIS PASTEUR
Famous French Speakers

1. He discovered that germs can cause a large number of illnesses.
2. Vaccination.
3. Rabies.
4. That it may make us think of the verb "pasteurise".
5. False - Louis Pasteur came up with the process of pasteurisation, which is why it is named after him.

ANAGRAMME 3
Jumbled Letters

I. **paresseux** - lazy

Here are some of the common words that can be made out of these letters:

- **aux** - at the, to the
- **eau(x)** (f) - water(s)
- **eux** - them
- **par** - by, through
- **pas** (m) - step
- **peu** - little
- **pur/e** - pure
- **rue(s)** (f) - street(s)
- **ses** - his, her, its
- **sur** - on
- **paru/e** (from **paraître**) - seemed
- **peau(x)** (f) - skin(s)
- **peur(s)** (f) - fear(s)
- **peux** (from **pouvoir**) - can
- **puer** - to stink
- **sera / seras** (from **être**) - will be
- **user** - to use, to wear out
- **pause** (f) - break, pause
- **repas** (m) - meal
- **Russe** (m/f) - Russian
- **russe** - Russian
- **super** - great, super

- **passer** - to pass
- **presse** (f) - press
- **paresse** (f) - laziness

2. **papillon** (m) - butterfly

- **ail** (m) - garlic
- **loi** (f) - law
- **lion** (m) - lion
- **loin** - far
- **pain** (m) - bread
- **paon** (m) - peacock
- **papi** (m) - granddad
- **plan** (m) - plan, map
- **poil** (m) - hair, fur
- **poli** - polite
- **alpin** - Alpine
- **appli** (f) - app
- **lapin** (m) - rabbit
- **piano** (m) - piano

DES PRIX
Number Focus

1. Les chaussures coûtent **quatre-vingt-douze euros**.
2. Je voudrais retirer **deux-cent-cinquante euros**.
3. Cette chemise coûte **soixante-dix-neuf euros**.
4. Je voudrais changer **trois-cent-vingt-cinq dollars** en francs suisses.
5. Ce manteau coûte **cent-dix-huit euros**.

6. Je voudrais changer **cinq-cent-soixante-sept livres** en euros.
7. Les billets sont à **quarante-quatre euros**.
8. Le taxi coûte **trente-six euros**.
9. Je voudrais changer **quatre-cent-trois euros** en livres.
10. Ça fait **quatre-vingt-un euros** en tout.

TAPENADE D'OLIVES NOIRES
Taste Bud Tantaliser

1. Il y a beaucoup trop de **poivre** dans cette soupe et je n'aime pas la nourriture épicée !
2. J'aime bien les cerises, mais je préfère les acheter déjà **dénoyautées**.
3. Hélène a marché **jusqu'à** la plage, mais quand il a commencé à pleuvoir elle a décidé de rentrer chez elle.
4. Maman m'a toujours dit de ne pas ajouter plus d'une **pincée** de sel dans un plat, parce que ce n'est pas bon pour la santé.
5. Heureusement, le réparateur de vélo m'a dit que la chaîne de vélo fonctionnait bien et qu'elle avait tout simplement besoin d'un peu d'**huile**.
6. Maintenant que j'habite à Madrid, j'améliore **progressivement** mon espagnol en parlant avec mes nouveaux voisins et avec les gens qui travaillent dans l'épicerie du coin.
7. Mélanie, tu prends une seule **cuillère** de sucre dans ton thé ou plus ?

8. À chaque fois que j'essaie de faire des croissants à la maison, ils n'ont jamais la forme **souhaitée**, mais ils sont délicieux quand même !

9. Tous les invités sont arrivés à l'heure, **sauf** Jean qui a manqué son train et qui est donc arrivé avec une demi-heure de retard.

10. Vous pensez qu'il serait possible d'**obtenir** ce livre avant lundi prochain ? J'en ai vraiment besoin.

DÉFI DE TRADUCTION 4
Translation Challenge

1. Anne s'est promenée avec sa sœur.

EXPLANATION:

- All reflexive verbs form the perfect tense with **être** as the auxiliary verb. This means that the past participle has to agree with the subject. Here, since the subject is feminine, the past participle takes an extra **-e**.

- Possessive adjectives must agree in gender and number with the noun they refer to. Therefore, **sa** agrees with **sœur**, which is a feminine singular noun.

2. Tu as / Vous avez vu ce film ? C'est génial / super / excellent !

EXPLANATION:

- Remember that the **passé composé** in French is used to translate both the past simple (for example, "did you see … ?") and the present perfect tense (for example, "have you seen … ?") in English.
- You could also say **as-tu vu ce film ? / avez-vous vu ce film ?** or **est-ce que tu as vu ce film ? / est-ce que vous avez vu ce film ?**
- When the noun is masculine and begins with a consonant, the word for "this" is **ce**.
- In a more informal context, **génial** and **super** are two common ways to say "great". **Excellent** could be heard in both formal and informal contexts.

3. J'ai faim. Allons au restaurant.

EXPLANATION:

- To say "let's do something" in French, we use the **nous** form of the imperative. For regular verbs, this is the same as the **nous** form of the verb in the present tense, but without the subject pronoun (**nous**): in this case **allons** from **aller**.
- When you combine the preposition **à** with the masculine definite article (**le**), then **à** + **le** becomes **au**.

4. Les voisins / Les voisines nous ont rendu visite lundi soir.

EXPLANATION:

- **Voisin/e** (m/f) is the word for "neighbour", giving us
  les voisins in the masculine plural form or, if the
  neighbours are all female, **les voisines**.
- In French, we use the verb **visiter** to talk about
  visiting a place, but when talking about visiting a
  person we use **rendre visite à quelqu'un**.
- The indirect object pronoun **nous**, meaning "to us",
  is placed before the auxiliary verb. Indirect object
  pronouns are used with verbs which take **à** as a
  preposition: in this case, **rendre visite à quelqu'un**
  ("to visit someone").
- In French, we can simply say **lundi soir** for "on
  Monday evening". We don't need a word for "on".

5. Mes parents se sont rencontrés quand ils avaient dix-sept
ans / à l'âge de dix-sept ans.

EXPLANATION:

- Possessive adjectives must agree in gender and
  number with the noun they refer to. Therefore, **mes**
  agrees with **parents**, which is a masculine plural
  noun.
- All reflexive verbs form the perfect tense with **être**
  as the auxiliary verb. This means that the past
  participle has to agree with the subject. Since the

subject is plural, the past participle takes an extra -s.

- In French, we use the verb **avoir** ("to have") rather than "to be" to indicate age. It may help to remember this by thinking of age as something that isn't permanent, as your age changes every year.

AMÉLIE MAURESMO
Famous French Speakers

1. At the age of four.
2. False - Mauresmo showed herself to be extremely talented throughout her youth and remained passionate about tennis from the age of four.
3. She made it to the final of the Australian Open.
4. She became the first French female tennis player of the modern era to be ranked as world number 1.
5. She became the second French female tennis player to be ranked as world number 1 in the history of women's tennis.

ANAGRAMME 4
Jumbled Letters

1. **atterrir** - to land

While there are many words that can be made out of these letters, here are some of the most common ones:

- **air** (m) - air, appearance

- **art** (m) - art
- **ira** (from **aller**) - will go
- **rat/e** (m/f) - rat
- **tir** (m) - shot
- **tri** (m) - sorting
- **rare** - rare
- **rire** - to laugh
- **rite** (m) - rite, ritual
- **rater** - to miss
- **taire** - to be quiet
- **tarte** (f) - tart
- **tirer** - to pull
- **titre** (m) - title
- **trait** (m) - trait
- **trier** - to separate, to sort
- **attirer** - to attract
- **retrait** (m) - withdrawal

2. **volontiers** - gladly, willingly

- **est** (from **être**) - is
- **est** (m) - east
- **ils** - they
- **les** - the
- **lit(s)** (m) - bed(s)
- **loi(s)** (f) - law(s)
- **nos** - our
- **oie(s)** (f) - goose / geese
- **ont** (from **avoir**) - have
- **roi(s)** (m) - king(s)

- **sel** (m) - salt
- **soi** - self
- **son** - his, her, its
- **tes** - your
- **toi** - you
- **ton** - your
- **ver(s)** (m) - worm(s)
- **vie(s)** (f) - life / lives
- **vin** (m) - wine
- **vol(s)** (m) - flight(s), theft(s)
- **vos** - your
- **ivre** - drunk
- **lent** - slow
- **lion(s)** (m) - lion(s)
- **lire** - to read
- **loin** - far
- **noir/e** - black
- **rien** - nothing
- **rose** (f) - rose
- **rose** - pink
- **soir** (m) - evening
- **sont** (from **être**) - are
- **vent(s)** (m) - wind(s)
- **vers** - towards
- **vert** - green
- **vite** - quickly
- **voir** - to see
- **vont** (from **aller**) - go
- **liste** (f) - list
- **livre(s)** (m) - book(s)

- **tenir** - to hold
- **tiers** (m) - third
- **trois** - three
- **venir** - to come
- **votre** - your
- **orteil(s)** (m) - toe(s)
- **violon(s)** (m) - violin(s)

À QUELLE HEURE ... ?
Number Focus

1. Je rentre à la maison à **dix-neuf heures**.
2. Nous dînons ensemble à **vingt heures**.
3. La fête commence à **vingt-et-une heures**.
4. Mes collègues déjeunent à **treize heures**.
5. Les enfants prennent le goûter à **seize heures**.
6. Le cours se termine à **dix-sept heures**.
7. On va voir un film à **quinze heures**.
8. Vous avez un rendez-vous à **quatorze heures**.
9. Le train arrive à **vingt-trois heures**.
10. Je vais me coucher à **vingt-deux heures**.

GRATIN DAUPHINOIS
Taste Bud Tantaliser

EXERCISE I - COMPREHENSION

1. FAUX - The first step is to chop the potatoes.
2. FAUX - The potatoes should be cut into thin slices.
3. VRAI

4. FAUX - The cheese is sprinkled over the top once the dish is full.

5. VRAI

EXERCISE 2 - FIND THE FRENCH

1. à chaque fois
2. le plat est rempli
3. disposez les lamelles
4. du gruyère râpé
5. en fines lamelles

15-MINUTE COFFEE BREAKS

CHECKLIST
15-MINUTE COFFEE BREAKS

Reading Focus

❏ Jeu de l'oie - page 166

❏ Moment cinéma social - page 185

❏ Annie Cordy - page 202

Guided Writing

❏ Voici Amandine - page 170

❏ Ma routine du matin - page 190

Vocabulary Consolidation

❏ En voyage - page 173

❏ Le monde du travail - page 194

❏ L'environnement et l'écologie - page 206

Grammar Focus

❏ Le passé composé - page 180

❏ Les verbes pronominaux - page 198

41

JEU DE L'OIE
READING FOCUS

Aimez-vous jouer à « Snakes and Ladders » ? In the text below, we learn about the French equivalent of this game: **le jeu de l'oie**, literally, "the game of the goose". Read the text and answer the comprehension and language questions that follow to test your understanding. You'll encounter some vocabulary specific to board games in this text, so you may need to use the vocabulary list to help you!

* * *

Avez-vous déjà joué au jeu de l'oie ? C'est un jeu de société de parcours qui date du 16e siècle. Le plateau est composé de 63 cases qui sont réparties en spirale et qui comprennent des pièges. Ce jeu de hasard peut se jouer dès l'âge de trois ans ! Chaque joueur lance les deux dés et avance son pion selon le nombre obtenu. Le but du jeu est d'être le premier à arriver à la dernière case. À vous de jouer !

VOCABULARY

oie (f) - goose
jeu (m) **de société** - board game
jeu (m) **de parcours** - racing game
siècle (m) - century
plateau (m) - board
case (f) - box
réparti/e - spread out
comprennent < comprendre - include < to include
piège (m) - trap
hasard (m) - luck, chance
peut se jouer - can be played
dès - (starting) from
lance < lancer - rolls < to roll
dé (m) - dice, die
pion (m) - piece, counter, pawn
obtenu < obtenir - got, obtained < to get, to obtain
but (m) - aim

EXERCISE 1 - COMPREHENSION

Answer the following questions in English.

1. What kind of game is **le jeu de l'oie?**

   ✎_____

   _____

2. How old is the game?

   ✎_____

   _____

3. How is the board laid out?

✎_____

_____

4. According to the text, how old do players have to be
   to participate?

   ✎_____

   _____

5. What is the aim of the game?

   ✎_____

   _____

EXERCISE 2 - TRANSLATE

Translate the following words or phrases from the text into
English.

1. dès l'âge de

   ✎_____

2. le plateau est composé de

   ✎_____

3. selon

   ✎_____

4. lancer un dé

   ✎_____

5. le but du jeu

   ✎_____

EXERCISE 3 - FIND THE FRENCH

Find the French in the text for the following words or phrases.

1. a board game
   ✎_____

2. a game of chance
   ✎_____

3. a piece
   ✎_____

4. the final box
   ✎_____

5. which contain traps
   ✎_____

* * *

Super travail ! Once you've had a go, turn to page 211 to check your answers.

42

VOICI AMANDINE
GUIDED WRITING

In this writing activity, the type of writing that we are focusing on is descriptions of people. Read the example text below, then use our suggested phrases to help you write your own text.

* * *

Amandine a trente-quatre ans et habite à Bruxelles. Elle travaille dans une maison d'édition de livres pour enfants. Elle a les cheveux mis-longs, blonds et raides. Elle porte des lunettes pour la lecture et pour conduire. Pendant son temps libre, elle adore lire, évidemment, mais elle s'occupe surtout de son fils, Adrien, qui a trois ans. Elle est mariée et son mari Christian est cuisinier. Elle aime bien le théâtre mais elle n'aime pas l'opéra. Le dimanche, elle fait des mots croisés. Quand il fait beau, elle fait de longues promenades en famille.

SUGGESTED PHRASES

il / elle a … ans - he / she is … years old

il / elle habite à … - he / she lives in …

il /elle a les cheveux courts / longs / blonds / roux / bruns / colorés - he / she has short / long / blonde / red / brown / dyed hair

il / elle porte des lunettes / un chapeau / un manteau - he / she wears glasses / a hat / a coat

il / elle travaille à / dans … - he / she works at / in …

il / elle est professeur/e / avocat/e / cuisinier/ière - he / she is a teacher / lawyer / cook

il / elle est célibataire / en couple / marié/e - he / she is single / in a relationship / married

pendant son temps libre - during his / her free time

ses passions / hobbys sont … - his / her passions / hobbies are …

il / elle aime / n'aime pas / préfère - he / she likes / doesn't like / prefers

C'est à vous ! Write a short paragraph like the one about Amandine. It can be about anyone you like: for example, a family member, a colleague or an imaginary person.

🖉_____

_____

_____

_____

_____

_____

_____

_____

_____

_____

_____

_____

_____

_____

_____

_____

_____

_____

_____

* * *

Bravo ! We hope that you've enjoyed practising your writing skills in this activity.

43

EN VOYAGE
VOCABULARY CONSOLIDATION

In this activity, we're going to practise some vocabulary on the topic of travel. We have chosen 20 words or phrases on this topic and have put together four exercises which will help you to familiarise yourself with this vocabulary. Make sure you've read through the list a few times, then cover it up with your hand or a piece of paper and try to complete the exercises that follow without looking. **Alors, c'est parti !**

* * *

l'agence (f) de voyages - travel agency
l'ambassade (f) - embassy
l'arrivée (f) - arrival
la carte d'embarquement - boarding pass, boarding card
la correspondance - connection
le décalage horaire - time difference
le départ - departure
être perdu/e - to be lost

faire du tourisme - to go sightseeing

faire sa valise - to pack one's suitcase

faire une croisière - to go on a cruise

l'itinéraire (m) - itinerary

loger à l'hôtel - to stay in a hotel

l'office (m) **de tourisme** - tourist information office

partir en vacances - to go on holiday, to go on vacation

le passeport - passport

le plan - map

prendre des photos - to take photos

le/la vacancier/ière - holidaymaker, vacationer

le voyage d'affaires - business trip

EXERCISE 1 - TRANSLATE

Write the French translation of these words or phrases.

1. itinerary

   ✎_____

2. to go on holiday / vacation

   ✎_____

3. travel agency

   ✎_____

4. to be lost

   ✎_____

5. to pack one's suitcase

   ✎_____

EXERCISE 2 - WHAT'S MISSING?

1. Take another look at the first five words and phrases in our list:

correspondance
ambassade
agence de voyages
carte d'embarquement
arrivée

Now, cover up the list above with your hand or a piece of paper and complete the list below with the one that's missing.

carte d'embarquement
ambassade
agence de voyages
correspondance
✎_____

2. Let's do the same with the next five words or phrases in the list:

décalage horaire
départ
faire du tourisme
être perdu/e
faire sa valise

Now, cover them up and spot what's missing from the list below:

> **décalage horaire**
> **faire sa valise**
> **être perdu/e**
> **départ**
> ✎ _____

3. Here are the next five:

> **office de tourisme**
> **itinéraire**
> **partir en vacances**
> **loger à l'hôtel**
> **faire une croisière**

Which one is missing from the following list?

> **itinéraire**
> **office de tourisme**
> **faire une croisière**
> **partir en vacances**
> ✎ _____

4. Here is the final list of five pieces of vocabulary:

> **voyage d'affaires**
> **prendre des photos**
> **passeport**

vacancier/ière

plan

Cover them up and fill in the gap with the missing word or phrase.

plan

voyage d'affaires

passeport

vacancier/ière

✎_____

EXERCISE 3 - ODD ONE OUT

1. Which *two* of the words or phrases from the list below would be unlikely to be used when talking about travelling for work?

faire sa valise

voyage d'affaires

faire une croisière

loger à l'hôtel

vacancier/ière

✎_____

✎_____

2. Which *three* of the following words or phrases would be unlikely to be used when talking about some friends from Marseille doing a road trip around France?

> correspondance
> plan
> itinéraire
> décalage horaire
> carte d'embarquement
> prendre des photos
> faire du tourisme

✎ _____

✎ _____

✎ _____

EXERCISE 4 - FILL IN THE GAPS

Fill in each gap with the most appropriate word or phrase from the list. **Attention** ! You may have to include the definite (**le**, **la** or **l'**) or indefinite (**un** or **une**) article. If you need to, you can refer back to the vocabulary list to help you.

1. ✎ _____ est une personne qui est en vacances ailleurs que chez elle.

2. Il y a ✎ _____ de six heures entre Paris et New York.

3. Quand François a perdu son ✎ _____ pendant ses

vacances en Australie, il a dû aller à

✎_____ de France à

Canberra.

4. Le premier jour de son séjour à Londres, Juliette est

allée à ✎_____ pour

trouver des informations sur les attractions

touristiques et pour acheter

✎_____ de la ville.

* * *

When you're ready, turn to page 212 to find the answers to the exercises.

44

LE PASSÉ COMPOSÉ
GRAMMAR FOCUS

In this Grammar Focus, we're going to practise using the perfect tense (**le passé composé**). Read the short explanation below to remind yourself how this tense works, then put this into practice by completing the exercises that follow.

* * *

The perfect tense is formed of the auxiliary verb **avoir** or **être** and a past participle. For example:

J'ai mangé un sandwich.
I ate a sandwich.

Elle est allée à la plage.
She went to the beach.

With verbs which take **être** as their auxiliary, the past participle has to agree with the subject. Since the subject in the second example above is feminine, an extra -e is added to the past participle.

Remember that all reflexive verbs also take **être** as their auxiliary verb. For example:

Les enfants se sont réveillés tôt.
The children woke up early.

Now, let's practise this. Have a go at the three exercises that follow and make sure to keep in mind what you just read.

EXERCISE 1 - PAST PARTICIPLES

Insert the past participle into the following sentences. The infinitive form of the verb is given in brackets. Watch out for the four verbs which have irregular past participles.

1. Nous avons ✎_____ [**danser**] toute la soirée.
2. Ma sœur est ✎_____ [**rentrer**] chez elle après la fête.
3. J'ai ✎_____ [**avoir**] une idée !
4. On a ✎_____ [**boire**] du café ce matin.
5. Alexandre a ✎_____ [**recevoir**] une lettre de sa mère.
6. Les étudiantes se sont ✎_____ [**coucher**] tôt hier soir.
7. Les voleurs sont ✎_____ [**partir**] en courant.

8. Tu as ✎_____ [**ranger**] tes affaires ?

9. Où avez-vous ✎_____ [**mettre**] les dossiers ?

10. La fête s'est ✎_____ [**terminer**] avant minuit.

EXERCISE 2 - REWRITE

Rewrite the following sentences in the perfect tense.

1. Je lis une histoire très intéressante.

   ✎_____

   _____

2. Le train arrive à l'heure.

   ✎_____

   _____

3. Ses amis viennent le voir.

   ✎_____

   _____

4. Nous aimons le film.

   ✎_____

   _____

5. Isabelle va en ville pour faire les courses.

   ✎_____

   _____

6. Ils se promènent dans le parc.

   ✎_____

   _____

7. Tu fais tes devoirs tout seul.

✎ _____

_____

8. Vous apprenez beaucoup de choses.

✎ _____

_____

9. On travaille ensemble sur ce projet.

✎ _____

_____

10. Elles se lèvent tôt aujourd'hui.

✎ _____

_____

EXERCISE 3 - COMPLETE THE SENTENCES

Look carefully at the past participles and circle the most appropriate subject to complete the following sentences.

1. **Jean / Marie / La femme** est parti sans dire au revoir.
2. **Sa fille / Son fils / Son cousin** s'est habillée rapidement.
3. **Ils / Les amies / Les amis** sont restées à la maison.
4. **Le chanteur / La chanteuse / L'actrice** est devenu très célèbre.
5. **Les Italiens / Les Anglaises / Les Françaises** sont revenus à l'hôtel.
6. **Cette pomme / Ce biscuit / Il** est tombée par terre.
7. **Il / Ma tante / François** est venue me rendre visite.

* * *

Très bon travail ! Once you've finished, turn to page 215 to find the answers to these exercises.

45

MOMENT CINÉMA SOCIAL
READING FOCUS

In this Reading Focus, we're taking a look at a text about an interesting French film. Once you've read through it, have a go at the comprehension questions and language exercises that follow. If you'd like an extra challenge, try reading the text and completing the exercises before looking at the vocabulary list, but remember it's always there if you need some help!

* * *

Un nouveau film est sorti en 2019. Il s'intitule *Les Misérables*. Pourtant il ne s'agit ni d'une adaptation du roman classique de Victor Hugo, ni de la comédie musicale hollywoodienne de 2012. En fait, il s'agit d'un film dramatique français qui parle de problèmes bien plus contemporains. C'est le premier long métrage de Ladj Ly, un réalisateur français d'origine malienne. L'histoire du film parle de tensions entre les policiers et les habitants d'un quartier défavorisé.

Lorsqu'une bagarre et un malentendu sont filmés par un drone, le drame commence. Voir ce film, c'est voir la France sous un autre angle, car on sort du cinéma avec le sentiment d'avoir eu une expérience importante et une vision différente.

VOCABULARY

est sorti < sortir - came out < to come out, to be released
s'intitule < s'intituler - is called < to be called, to be titled
pourtant - yet
il ne s'agit ni de ... ni de ... - it is neither ... nor ...
roman (m) - novel
comédie (f) **musicale** - musical
hollywoodien/ne - (of) Hollywood
bien plus - much more
contemporain/e - contemporary
long métrage (m) - feature-length film
réalisateur (m) - director
d'origine malienne - of Malian origin
quartier (m) **défavorisé** - disadvantaged area
bagarre (f) - fight
drame (m) - drama
sous un autre angle - from another angle
le sentiment d'avoir eu - the feeling of having had

EXERCISE 1 - COMPREHENSION

Answer the following questions in English.

1. What event took place in 2019?

   ✎ _____

   _____

2. True or false: the film discussed in the text is an adaptation of a novel by Victor Hugo.

   ✎ _____

   _____

3. How many feature films had Ladj Ly directed before *Les Misérables*?

   ✎ _____

   _____

4. The topic of the film is the tensions between which two groups?

   ✎ _____

   _____

5. According to the text, why can seeing this film be thought of as allowing the viewer to see France from another angle?

   ✎ _____

   _____

EXERCISE 2 - VERB SEARCH

There are 10 different verbs used in the text. Note them down on the lines on the next page and give their infinitive form.

All of the verbs appear in the present tense or in their infinitive form except for one. Can you spot which one it is and name the tense in which it appears?

1. ✎_____
2. ✎_____
3. ✎_____
4. ✎_____
5. ✎_____
6. ✎_____
7. ✎_____
8. ✎_____
9. ✎_____
10. ✎_____

EXERCISE 3 - FIND THE FRENCH

Find the French in the text for the following words or phrases.

1. it is called

   ✎_____

2. neither ... nor ...

   ✎_____

3. the story of the film deals with

   ✎_____

4. when

   ✎_____

5. you come out of the cinema

   ✎_____

* * *

Once you've finished all three exercises, you can turn to page 217 to check your answers.

46

MA ROUTINE DU MATIN
GUIDED WRITING

In this activity, you'll have the chance to practise your writing skills. Below is an example text on the topic of morning routine. Read it through to give you some ideas, then use the suggested phrases on the next page to help you write your own paragraph about your morning routine. **Allez, on y va !**

* * *

Le matin, mon réveil sonne à 7h. Je m'étire un peu avant de sortir de mon lit. Quand je me lève, je descends dans la cuisine pour préparer mon café. Je bois d'abord un grand verre d'eau, puis un café serré en lisant quelques pages d'un livre. Je me change en habits de sport et je vais courir 15 minutes avec mon chien. Il est toujours content de sortir. Une fois que j'ai fini mon sport, je donne à manger à mon chien, j'allume la radio et je me brosse les dents. Je prends une douche, puis je choisis mes vêtements de la journée et je m'habille. Je redescends dans la cuisine pour manger un fruit et un morceau de pain. À 8h45, je prends la voiture pour aller au bureau.

SUGGESTED PHRASES

mon réveil sonne à ... heures - my alarm goes off at ... o'clock

je me réveille à ... heures - I wake up at ... o'clock

je me lève à ... heures - I get up at ... o'clock

d'abord / avant tout - firstly / before anything else

avant de me laver / de m'habiller / de partir - before washing / getting dressed / leaving

je fais du sport - I exercise

je prépare mon café / mon petit-déjeuner / mon repas de midi - I make my coffee / my breakfast / my lunch

en lisant mes e-mails / en écoutant la radio / en regardant les nouvelles - while I read my emails / while I listen to the radio / while I watch the news

une fois que j'ai fait ... je ... - once I have done ... I ...

je mange du pain / des œufs / des fruits / des céréales - I eat bread / eggs / fruit / cereal

je pars à ... heures - I leave at ... o'clock

je prends la voiture / le train / le métro - I take the car / the train / the metro

À **vous la parole** ! Now it's your turn to describe your morning routine or, alternatively, what your ideal morning routine would be like!

_____

* * *

Bravo ! We hope that you've enjoyed practising your writing skills in this activity.

47

LE MONDE DU TRAVAIL
VOCABULARY CONSOLIDATION

This activity is all about practising and consolidating vocabulary. The list below contains 20 words or phrases on the topic of work. Take a couple of minutes to familiarise yourself with the vocabulary, then cover up the list with your hand or a piece of paper and try to complete the exercises on the next few pages without looking at it. **Bonne chance !**

* * *

à temps partiel - part-time
à temps plein - full-time
la carrière - career
le congé de maternité / paternité - maternity / paternity leave
démissionner - to resign
embaucher - to hire, to take on
l'entretien (m) - interview
être au chômage - to be unemployed

faire du télétravail - to work from home
faire la navette - to commute
le jour de congé - day off
licencier - to dismiss
le/la patron/ne - boss
la pause déjeuner - lunch break
poser sa candidature - to apply
le poste - post, position
la retraite - retirement
la réunion - meeting
le stage en entreprise - internship
travailler de nuit - to work nights, to work the night shift

EXERCISE 1 - TRANSLATE

Cover up the vocabulary list and write down the French translation of the words and phrases below.

1. to apply

   ✎_____

2. internship

   ✎_____

3. full-time

   ✎_____

4. to resign

   ✎_____

5. paternity leave

   ✎_____

EXERCISE 2 - MISSING LETTERS

Fill in the missing letters to make words from the list on the topic of work.

1. _ a r _ _ è r e
2. l _ c e _ c _ _ r
3. e _ _ r e t _ e n
4. _ o s _ e
5. e m _ a _ c _ e r

EXERCISE 3 - DEFINITIONS

Identify the word or phrase being described in each of the following definitions.

1. travailler à la maison

   _____

2. voyager à son lieu de travail

   _____

3. ne pas avoir de travail

   _____

4. la personne qui est responsable d'une équipe ou d'une entreprise

   _____

5. un jour où on n'a pas besoin de travailler

   _____

EXERCISE 4 - FILL IN THE GAPS

Fill in each gap with the most appropriate word or phrase from the list. Feel free to refer back to the list to help you with some of the trickier ones.

1. Je prends la ✎_____ tous les jours à 12h30 et je mange dans un café avec mes collègues.

2. Mon fils fait ses études à l'université en ce moment, mais il travaille ✎_____ aussi pour gagner un peu d'argent.

3. Chaque lundi à 9h30 il y a une ✎_____ avec tous les employés pour organiser les tâches de la semaine.

4. Le jour de ses soixante ans, Hélène a décidé de prendre sa ✎_____ .

5. Quant Hervé travaillait ✎_____ , il se couchait à 7h et se réveillait à 15h.

***

Excellent travail ! The answers to these exercises can be found on page 218.

48

LES VERBES PRONOMINAUX
GRAMMAR FOCUS

In this grammar activity, we are looking at reflexive verbs. Read the short explanation below, then have a go at the three exercises that follow. **Bonne chance !**

*** * ***

Reflexive verbs are verbs which are formed with a reflexive pronoun, as the subject is doing the action to itself. Many verbs that are used to describe daily routine are reflexive. Let's take a look at an example of the conjugation of a French reflexive verb, using **se laver**, meaning "to wash (oneself)":

je me lave - I wash (myself)
tu te laves - you wash (yourself)
il/elle se lave - he/she washes (himself/herself)
nous nous lavons - we wash (ourselves)
vous vous lavez - you wash (yourselves)
ils/elles se lavent - they wash (themselves)

Note that for reflexive verbs beginning with a vowel or a silent **h-**, **me** becomes **m'**, **te** becomes **t'** and **se** becomes **s'**.

Allez, c'est à vous ! Let's practise using reflexive verbs in these three exercises.

EXERCISE 1 - MATCH

Match each of the reflexive verbs with its English translation.

> **se réveiller | se lever | s'habiller |**
> **se laver | se coucher | se raser | s'appeler |**
> **se doucher | se maquiller | se reposer**

1. to be called
   _____

2. to get up
   _____

3. to wash
   _____

4. to shave
   _____

5. to shower
   _____

6. to get dressed
   _____

7. to put on make-up
   _____

8. to rest
   _____

9. to wake up

   ✎_____

10. to go to bed

    ✎_____

EXERCISE 2 - ADD THE PRONOUN

Complete the following sentences with the correct reflexive pronoun.

1. À quelle heure est-ce que tu ✎_____ lèves ?
2. Il ne ✎_____ réveille jamais à l'heure !
3. Elle ✎_____ assied sur la chaise à côté de la fenêtre.
4. Nous allons ✎_____ baigner dans la mer.
5. Je ✎_____ brosse les dents après le dîner.
6. Ils ✎_____ lavent les mains avant de manger.
7. Elles ✎_____ appellent comment ?
8. Vous ✎_____ maquillez tous les jours ?
9. Ils ✎_____ couchent à minuit.
10. Je ✎_____ inquiète pour ma sœur.

EXERCISE 3 - THE PERFECT TENSE

All reflexive verbs form the perfect tense with **être** as the auxiliary verb. This means that the past participle has to agree with the subject of the verb.

For each sentence below, conjugate the reflexive verb given in brackets in the perfect tense. Take care to use the correct reflexive pronoun.

1. Elle ✎_____
   [**se réveiller**] à sept heures.

2. Elles ✎_____
   [**s'habiller**] de la même manière.

3. Julie et Pierre ✎_____
   [**se marier**] en printemps.

4. Nous ✎_____
   [**se promener**] dans le parc.

5. Mon fils ✎_____
   [**se doucher**] avant de partir.

6. Tu ✎_____ [**se coucher**]
   très tard.

7. Ils ✎_____ [**s'arrêter**]
   devant la maison.

8. Vous ✎_____ [**se lever**] à
   la même heure.

9. Je ✎_____ [**se reposer**]
   pendant les vacances.

10. Il ✎_____ [**se raser**]
    devant le miroir.

* * *

Once you've finished, turn to page 220 to check your answers.

49

ANNIE CORDY
READING FOCUS

In this reading activity, we'll be focusing on a text about one of Belgium's most well-known personalities. Once you've read through it, have a go at the comprehension questions and language exercises that follow to test your understanding. **Bonne lecture !**

* * *

En septembre 2020, la Belgique a dû dire au revoir à l'un de ses artistes préférés. Annie Cordy était une chanteuse, danseuse et actrice. Née en 1928 à Bruxelles, elle a donc bercé le monde francophone de chansons pendant des décennies ! Elle est décédée à l'âge de 92 ans en France et laisse derrière elle plus de 700 chansons avec son style tellement positif et entraînant. On retient d'elle un sourire jusqu'aux oreilles, une énergie éclatante, et des collaborations avec les plus grands artistes du 20ᵉ siècle.

VOCABULARY

a dû < devoir - had to < to have to
bercé < bercer - lulled < to lull, to accompany (with music)
décennie (f) - decade
décédé/e < décéder - died < to die
entraînant/e - upbeat, catchy
retient < retenir - holds on to < to hold on to, to remember
oreille (f) - ear
éclatant/e - bursting, vibrant

EXERCISE 1 - COMPREHENSION

Answer the questions in English.

1. What happened in September 2020?
   🖎_____
   _____

2. Who was Annie Cordy?
   🖎_____
   _____

3. Why is Brussels mentioned?
   🖎_____
   _____

4. What were Annie Cordy's songs like?
   🖎_____
   _____

5. What will she be remembered for?
   🖎_____
   _____

EXERCISE 2 - SEARCH

In the text, find an example of each of the following:

1. a verb in the present tense
   ✎_____

2. a verb in the imperfect tense
   ✎_____

3. a verb in the perfect tense, using the auxiliary verb
   avoir
   ✎_____

4. a verb in the perfect tense, using the auxiliary verb
   être
   ✎_____

5. an adjective in its masculine singular form
   ✎_____

6. an adjective in its feminine singular form
   ✎_____

7. a masculine singular noun
   ✎_____

8. a feminine singular noun
   ✎_____

EXERCISE 3 - FIND THE FRENCH

Find the French translation of each of the following phrases from the text. Note that they don't appear in the order given below.

1. born in

   ✎_____

2. a smile from ear to ear

   ✎_____

3. had to say goodbye

   ✎_____

4. she will be remembered for

   ✎_____

* * *

When you're ready, you can find the answers on page 221.

L'ENVIRONNEMENT ET L'ÉCOLOGIE
VOCABULARY CONSOLIDATION

This activity will help you to get to know some vocabulary on the topic of the environment. Take some time to read through the vocabulary list, then cover it up with your hand or a piece of paper and try to complete the exercises that follow without referring to the list. **Bonne chance !**

* * *

l'arbre (m) - tree
les déchets (m, pl) - waste
la déforestation - deforestation
durable - sustainable
écoresponsable - environmentally friendly
l'énergie (f) **renouvelable** - renewable energy
la forêt tropicale - rainforest
les gaz (m, pl) **à effet de serre** - greenhouse gases
la mer - sea

nocif/ive - harmful
la plante - plant
planter - to plant
le plastique - plastic
la pollution - pollution
protéger - to protect
le reboisement / la reforestation - reforestation
le réchauffement climatique - global warming
recycler - to recycle
la rivière - river
la Terre - Earth

EXERCISE 1 - TRANSLATE

Cover up the vocabulary list and translate the following words and phrases into French.

1. to recycle
   ✎ _____

2. sustainable
   ✎ _____

3. waste
   ✎ _____

4. renewable energy
   ✎ _____

5. harmful
   ✎ _____

EXERCISE 2 - CATEGORISE

Have another look at the vocabulary from our list laid out below – this time, without the English translations – and sort the words according to their function.

arbre | déchets | déforestation | durable |
écoresponsable | énergie renouvelable | forêt tropicale |
gaz à effet de serre | mer | nocif/ive | plante |
planter | plastique | pollution | protéger |
reboisement/reforestation | réchauffement climatique |
recycler | rivière | Terre

NOUNS:

✎_____   _____
_____   _____
_____   _____
_____   _____
_____   _____
_____   _____
_____

VERBS:

✎_____   _____
_____   _____
_____   _____
_____   _____

_____   _____
_____   _____
_____   _____
_____

ADJECTIVES:

✎_____   _____
_____   _____
_____   _____
_____   _____
_____   _____
_____   _____
_____

EXERCISE 3 - COMPLETE THE SENTENCE

Circle the correct option to complete each sentence so that it makes sense.

1. La forêt amazonienne est en grand danger à cause de **la déforestation / la forêt tropicale.**
2. Une façon d'avoir un mode de vie plus **nocif / écoresponsable** est d'adopter un régime à base **d'arbres / de plantes.**
3. **Le reboisement / Le réchauffement climatique** est le résultat des émissions **de déchets / de gaz à effet de serre.**
4. Dans certaines villes, il y a maintenant des

restrictions de circulation pour réduire **la pollution /
le plastique** de l'air en ville.

5. Tout le monde peut agir pour protéger **les déchets /
la Terre.**

* * *

Once you're happy with your answers, turn to page 222 to
check them.

ANSWERS
15-MINUTE COFFEE BREAKS

JEU DE L'OIE
Reading Focus

EXERCISE 1 - COMPREHENSION

1. It's a board game and the game is a race.
2. Around 500 years old (dating from the 16th Century).
3. The board contains 63 boxes which are spread out in the shape of a spiral.
4. 3 years old.
5. To be the first player to reach the final box.

EXERCISE 2 - TRANSLATE

1. from the age of
2. the board is composed of / made up of / consists of
3. according to
4. to roll a die / dice

5. the aim of the game

1. un jeu de société
2. un jeu de hasard
3. un pion
4. la dernière case
5. qui comprennent des pièges

EN VOYAGE
Vocabulary Consolidation

1. itinéraire
2. partir en vacances
3. agence de voyages
4. être perdu/e
5. faire sa valise

1. **arrivée** ("arrival")
2. **faire du tourisme** ("to go sightseeing")
3. **loger à l'hôtel** ("to stay in a hotel")
4. **prendre des photos** ("to take photos")

EXERCISE 3 - ODD ONE OUT

1. faire une croisière, vacancier/ière

EXPLANATION:

The following three phrases could be used within the context of travelling for work:

> **faire sa valise** - to pack one's suitcase
> **voyage d'affaires** - business trip
> **loger à l'hôtel** - to stay in a hotel

The other two, however, would be more likely to be used when talking about travelling for a holiday:

> **faire une croisière** - to go on a cruise
> **vacancier/ière** - holidaymaker, vacationer

2. correspondance, décalage horaire, carte d'embar-quement

EXPLANATION:

The following three words or phrases could be used to describe a holiday road trip:

> **plan** - map
> **itinéraire** - itinerary
> **faire du tourisme** - to go sightseeing

The other three do not fit into this context:

- **correspondance** - connection. This term refers to a change or connection when travelling by rail, bus or aeroplane, for example, and is therefore not relevant when travelling by car.
- **décalage horaire** - time difference. As the friends are from Marseille and are on holiday in the same country, which is all in the same time zone, there would be no time difference involved in their travels.
- **carte d'embarquement** - boarding pass, boarding card. This term refers to a flight boarding pass and is therefore not relevant when travelling by car.

EXERCISE 4 - FILL IN THE GAPS

1. **Un vacancier / Une vacancière** est une personne qui est en vacances ailleurs que chez elle.
   TRANSLATION: *A holidaymaker (vacationer) is a person who is on holiday away from their home.*
2. Il y a **un décalage horaire** de six heures entre Paris et New York.
   TRANSLATION: *There is a time difference of six hours between Paris and New York.*
3. Quand François a perdu son **passeport** pendant ses vacances en Australie, il a dû aller à **l'ambassade** de France à Canberra.
   TRANSLATION: *When François lost his passport during his holiday in Australia, he had to go to the French embassy in Canberra.*

4. Le premier jour de son séjour à Londres, Juliette est allée à **l'office de tourisme** pour trouver des informations sur les attractions touristiques et pour acheter **un plan** de la ville.

TRANSLATION. *On the first day of her stay in London, Juliette went to the tourist information office to find information about the tourist attractions and to buy a map of the city.*

LE PASSÉ COMPOSÉ
Grammar Focus

EXERCISE 1 - PAST PARTICIPLES

1. Nous avons **dansé** toute la soirée.
2. Ma sœur est **rentrée** chez elle après la fête.
3. J'ai **eu** une idée !
4. On a **bu** du café ce matin.
5. Alexandre a **reçu** une lettre de sa mère.
6. Les étudiantes se sont **couchées** tôt hier soir.
7. Les voleurs sont **partis** en courant.
8. Tu as **rangé** tes affaires ?
9. Où avez-vous **mis** les dossiers ?
10. La fête s'est **terminée** avant minuit.

EXERCISE 2 - REWRITE

1. **J'ai lu** une histoire très intéressante.
2. Le train **est arrivé** à l'heure.
3. Ses amis **sont venus** le voir.

4. Nous **avons aimé** le film.

5. Isabelle **est allée** en ville pour faire les courses.

6. Ils **se sont promenés** dans le parc.

7. Tu **as fait** tes devoirs tout seul.

8. Vous **avez appris** beaucoup de choses.

9. On **a travaillé** ensemble sur ce projet.

10. Elles **se sont levées** tôt aujourd'hui.

EXERCISE 3 - COMPLETE THE SENTENCES

1. **Jean** est parti sans dire au revoir.
   EXPLANATION: The past participle **parti** is in its masculine singular form and Jean is the only masculine singular subject out of our three options.

2. **Sa fille** s'est habillée rapidement.
   EXPLANATION: The past participle **habillée** is in its feminine singular form.

3. **Les amies** sont restées à la maison.
   EXPLANATION: The past participle **restées** is in its feminine plural form.

4. **Le chanteur** est devenu très célèbre.
   EXPLANATION: The past participle **devenu** is in its masculine singular form.

5. **Les Italiens** sont revenus à l'hôtel.
   EXPLANATION: The past participle **revenus** is in its masculine plural form.

6. **Cette pomme** est tombée par terre.
   EXPLANATION: The past participle **tombée** is in its feminine singular form.

7. **Ma tante** est venue me rendre visite.

EXPLANATION: The past participle **venue** is in its feminine singular form.

MOMENT CINÉMA SOCIAL
Reading Focus

EXERCISE 1 - COMPREHENSION

1. A new film came out, which was called *Les Misérables*.
2. False - The text states that this film is neither an adaptation of Victor Hugo's classic novel, nor the 2012 Hollywood musical.
3. Zero. This was Ladj Ly's first feature-length film.
4. The police and the inhabitants of disadvantaged areas.
5. Because the viewer leaves the cinema with the feeling of having had an important experience and seen a different perspective.

EXERCISE 2 - VERB SEARCH

1. **est sorti < sortir** - perfect tense / **passé composé**
2. **s'intitule < s'intituler**
3. **s'agit < s'agir**
4. **parle < parler**
5. **est < être**
6. **sont < être**
7. **commence < commencer**
8. **voir**

9. **sort < sortir**
10. **avoir**

1. il s'intitule
2. ne ... ni ... ni ...
3. l'histoire du film parle de
4. lorsque
5. on sort du cinéma

LE MONDE DU TRAVAIL
Vocabulary Consolidation

1. poser sa candidature
2. stage en entreprise
3. à temps plein
4. démissionner
5. congé de paternité

1. **carrière** ("career")
2. **licencier** ("to dismiss")
3. **entretien** ("interview")
4. **poste** ("post")
5. **embaucher** ("to hire")

EXERCISE 3 - DEFINITIONS

1. **faire du télétravail** ("to work from home")
2. **faire la navette** ("to commute")
3. **ëtre au chömage** ("to be unemployed")
4. **le/la patron/ne** ("the boss")
5. **un jour de congé** ("a day off")

EXERCISE 4 - FILL IN THE GAPS

1. Je prends la **pause déjeuner** tous les jours à 12h30 et je mange dans un café avec mes collègues.
   TRANSLATION: *I take my lunch break every day at 12:30pm and I eat in a café with my colleagues.*
2. Mon fils fait ses études à l'université en ce moment, mais il travaille **à temps partiel** aussi pour gagner un peu d'argent.
   TRANSLATION: *My son is studying at university at the moment, but he also works part-time to earn a bit of money.*
3. Chaque lundi à 9h30 il y a une **réunion** avec tous les employés pour organiser les tâches de la semaine.
   TRANSLATION: *Every Monday at 9:30am there is a meeting with all the employees to organise the tasks of the week.*
4. Le jour de ses soixante ans, Hélène a décidé de prendre sa **retraite**.
   TRANSLATION: *On the day of her 60th birthday, Hélène decided to retire.*
5. Quant Hervé travaillait **de nuit**, il se couchait à 7h et

se réveillait à 15h.

TRANSLATION: *When Hervé was on the night shift, he went to bed at 7am and got up at 3pm.*

LES VERBES PRONOMINAUX
Grammar Focus

EXERCISE I - MATCH

1. s'appeler
2. se lever
3. se laver
4. se raser
5. se doucher
6. s'habiller
7. se maquiller
8. se reposer
9. se réveiller
10. se coucher

EXERCISE 2 - ADD THE PRONOUN

1. À quelle heure est-ce que tu **te** lèves ?
2. Il ne **se** réveille jamais à l'heure !
3. Elle **s'**assied sur la chaise à côté de la fenêtre.
4. Nous allons **nous** baigner dans la mer.
5. Je **me** brosse les dents après le dîner.
6. Ils **se** lavent les mains avant de manger.
7. Elles **s'**appellent comment ?
8. Vous **vous** maquillez tous les jours ?

9. Ils **se** couchent à minuit.

10. Je **m'**inquiète pour ma sœur.

1. Elle **s'est réveillée** à sept heures.

2. Elles **se sont habillées** de la même manière.

3. Julie et Pierre **se sont mariés** en printemps.

4. Nous **nous sommes promenés/ées** dans le parc.

5. Mon fils **s'est douché** avant de partir.

6. Tu **t'es couché/e** très tard.

7. Ils **se sont arrêtés** devant la maison.

8. Vous **vous êtes levés/ées** à la même heure.

9. Je **me suis reposé/e** pendant les vacances.

10. Il **s'est rasé** devant le miroir.

ANNIE CORDY
Reading Focus

EXERCISE I - COMPREHENSION

1. Annie Cordy, one of Belgium's favourite artists, died.

2. A singer, dancer and actor.

3. Because Annie Cordy was born there.

4. Positive / cheerful and upbeat / lively.

5. Her big smile from ear to ear, her vibrant energy and her collaborations with the greatest artists of the 20th Century.

EXERCISE 2 - SEARCH

1. laisse < laisser | retient < retenir
2. était < être
3. a dû < devoir | a (donc) bercé < bercer
4. est décédée < décéder
5. francophone | positif | entraînant
6. éclatante
7. monde | âge | style | sourire | siècle
8. chanteuse | danseuse | actrice | énergie

EXERCISE 3 - FIND THE FRENCH

1. née en
2. un sourire jusqu'aux oreilles
3. a dû dire au revoir
4. on retient d'elle

L'ENVIRONNEMENT ET L'ÉCOLOGIE
Vocabulary Consolidation

EXERCISE I - TRANSLATE

1. recycler
2. durable
3. déchets
4. énergie renouvelable
5. nocif/ive

EXERCISE 2 - CATEGORISE

NOUNS:

- **arbre** (m) - tree
- **déchets** (m, pl) - waste
- **déforestation** (f) - deforestation
- **énergie** (f) **renouvelable** - renewable energy
- **forêt** (f) **tropicale** - rainforest
- **gaz** (m, pl) **à effet de serre** - greenhouse gases
- **mer** (f) - sea
- **plante** (f) - plant
- **plastique** (m) - plastic
- **pollution** (f) - pollution
- **reboisement** (m) / **reforestation** (f) - reforestation
- **réchauffement** (m) **climatique** - global warming
- **rivière** (f) - river
- **Terre** (f) - Earth

VERBS:

- **planter** - to plant
- **protéger** - to protect
- **recycler** - to recycle

ADJECTIVES:

- **durable** - sustainable
- **écoresponsable** - environmentally friendly
- **nocif/ive** - harmful

EXERCISE 3 - COMPLETE THE SENTENCE

1. La forêt amazonienne est en grand danger à cause de
   la déforestation.
   TRANSLATION: *The Amazon rainforest is in great danger
   because of deforestation.*

2. Une façon d'avoir un mode de vie plus
   écoresponsable est d'adopter un régime à base **de
   plantes.**
   TRANSLATION: *One way of having a more environmentally
   responsible lifestyle is by adopting a plant-based diet.*

3. **Le réchauffement climatique** est le résultat des
   émissions **de gaz à effet de serre.**
   TRANSLATION: *Global warming is the result of
   greenhouse gas emissions.*

4. Dans certaines villes, il y a maintenant des
   restrictions de circulation pour réduire **la pollution**
   de l'air en ville.
   TRANSLATION: *In some cities, there are now traffic
   restrictions to reduce air pollution in the city.*

5. Tout le monde peut agir pour protéger **la Terre.**
   TRANSLATION: *Everyone can do something to protect the
   Earth.*

COFFEE BREAK LESSONS

CoffeeBreak
French

This is an index including some of the language and grammar points that are covered in this book, listed in alphabetical order and indicating where you can find a more detailed explanation in our Coffee Break French lessons. Search for "Coffee Break French" on Spotify, Apple Podcasts or wherever you get your podcasts to find the free versions of these audio lessons, or visit coffeebreakfrench.com to find out about our full courses.

* * *

First of all, here is a brief explanation of the abbreviations used and the courses mentioned:

CBF S1
Coffee Break French Season 1: our 40-lesson course
for beginners

CBF S2
Coffee Break French Season 2: our 40-lesson course for lower intermediate learners

CBF S3
Coffee Break French Season 3: our 40-lesson course for upper intermediate learners

CBF S4
Coffee Break French Season 4: our 40-lesson course for advanced learners

CBF Magazine
our 10-lesson Magazine series for intermediate learners

CBF En Route
our 10-lesson series for upper intermediate to advanced learners, recorded on location in the south of France

E1, E2, E3 ...
Episode 1, Episode 2, Episode 3 ...

* * *

We cover a number of topics in each lesson of Coffee Break French, but on the next page you can find out which lessons include a discussion about the following topics which feature in this book.

A

adjectives - *CBF S1 E8 & E18, CBF S2 E8*

adjectives (demonstrative) - *CBF S2 E19*

adjectives (possessive) - *CBF S1 E5 & E28, CBF S3 E15*

adjectives (which precede the noun) - *CBF S2 E9, CBF S3 E22*

adverbs (in the perfect tense) - *CBF S3 E1*

agreement of numbers - *CBF Magazine S1 E1*

après + **avoir/être** + past participle - *CBF S2 E27, CBF S3 E10, CBF S4 E5*

avant de + infinitive - *CBF S2 E26, CBF S3 E2*

C

the conditional - *CBF S2 E36, CBF S3 E25*

D

daily routine (topic) - *CBF S2 E2*

demonstrative adjectives - *CBF S2 E19*

direct object pronouns - *CBF S2 E31, CBF S3 E19, CBF S4 E14*

du, de la, de l' (partitive articles) - *CBF S1 E14, CBF S2 E12*

E

en (pronoun) - *CBF S1 E35, CBF S2 E21*

F

the future (immediate) - *CBF S2 E11 & E12*

the future tense - *CBF S2 E37, CBF S3 E2, E5 & E6, CBF S4 E17*

H

health, pains & ailments (topic) - *CBF S1 E28 & E29*

pronouns (relative) - *CBF S2 E25, CBF S3 E10 & E19, CBF S4 E39*
pronoun **en** - *CBF S1 E35, CBF S2 E21*
pronoun **y** - *CBF S2 E21*

Q
questions - *CBF S1 E11 & E22, CBF S2 E5, E6 & E28, CBF S3 E25, CBF S4 E13*

R
reflexive verbs - *CBF S2 E3*
reflexive verbs (in the perfect tense) - *CBF S2 E18*
relative pronouns - *CBF S2 E25, CBF S3 E10 & E19, CBF S4 E39*

V
venir de + infinitive - *CBF S2 E26*

Y
y (pronoun) - *CBF S2 E21*

ACKNOWLEDGEMENTS

This book has very much been a team effort and I would like to take the opportunity to thank the people who have helped to put it together.

Firstly, thanks to Sarah Cole, Chloe West, Emma Green and the whole team at Teach Yourself. It's been a pleasure to work with you all and we'd like to thank you for your belief in the project and your enthusiasm for helping us bring Coffee Break to a new audience around the world.

Un grand merci to our team of writers and proof readers, Sophie Giaux, Pierre-Benoît Hériaud and Susanna Naismith, who came up with all of the ideas and wrote the texts and exercises to help you practise your French.

We'd like to thank Maurizio Verducci, whose tireless research and expert advice has helped *50 French Coffee Breaks* see the light of day.

Merci infiniment to Ava Dinwoodie, our Series Editor. In addition to her role in the team of writers and proof readers, her dedication to the project and expert coordination meant that everyone knew exactly what they were doing and when it needed to be done!

Finally, thank you for reading the book and we very much hope you have enjoyed building your skills in French with us.

You may recall my mention of jazz virtuoso Charlie Parker in the Introduction to this book who, by focusing on practice, practice, practice, was then ready to fly and enjoy his performance. I hope that you're now feeling ready to let go and incorporate the new vocabulary, expressions and grammatical structures into your French on a daily basis.

Mark Pentleton - Founder, Coffee Break Languages

SHARE YOUR THOUGHTS

If you'd like to help other learners like yourself discover Coffee Break French, we'd be very grateful if you would consider leaving an honest review. If you bought the book online, you can do this easily by going to the website where you found it.

Merci beaucoup ! Thank you for sharing your thoughts and for helping other learners practise their French on their Coffee Break.

KEEP IN TOUCH

If you'd like to keep in touch with us and continue practising your French on your Coffee Break, just search for Coffee Break French on Facebook, Twitter, Instagram and YouTube.

We also send a monthly email newsletter to our learners, in which you can benefit from tips and tricks to help you with your language learning, along with links, useful resources and news of our latest releases. Visit coffeebreaklanguages.com/newsletter to sign up.

À bientôt !

facebook.com/coffeebreakfrench

twitter.com/learnfrench

instagram.com/coffeebreaklanguages

youtube.com/coffeebreaklanguages

NOTES

NOTES

NOTES

NOTES

NOTES

NOTES

NOTES

NOTES

NOTES

NOTES

NOTES

ALSO BY COFFEE BREAK LANGUAGES

Are you also learning another language? Or do you have a friend or relative who's a learner of a different language? Our *50 Coffee Breaks* series also includes books in Italian, German and Spanish, available both in paperback and as ebooks.

A presto, bis bald and **¡hasta pronto!**